RENAL DIET

The Low Sodium, Low Potassium, Healthy Kidney Cookbook

JOSH OLSEN

TABLE OF CONTENTS

WHAT IS CHRONIC DISEASE?

(CKD). A renal diet is one that limits the amount of sodium, protein, potassium, phosphorus and animal protein. It contains less than 60 g of total solids per day to help decrease the amount of fluid retained by the body. This diet also includes more fluids during meals to dilute this food intake in order to help avoid problems from too much salt intake.

Normal kidney function depends on healthy blood vessels, which deliver nutrients to the cells, and remove waste products from the blood. When these blood vessels are not working properly, waste products can build up in your blood. This leaky blood vessel problem is called "hypertension" (high blood pressure). The excess fluid (edema) can swell the feet, ankles, or abdomen with fluid. Swelling in the tissue outside of the kidneys can also occur; this is called "ascites" and may cause problems breathing if it becomes severe. Other indications that may be experienced are queasiness and vomiting, weight gain or loss without trying, weakness and fatigue, burning while urinating or feeling like you have to urinate often.

HOW TO HANDLE CHRONIC DISEASES

Normally the concern of a person with chronic disease ought to be the best way to manage it. By the time a disease is termed chronic, it normally will have failed normal treatment; leaving the person to learn how to live with the condition.

For that reason, anyone with kidney disease, for example, should focus on slowing down any damage to the kidneys. Every disease has fundamental cause or contributing factor; and it is important that this cause be identified by a professional, so that it can be targeted for control. If a person does not seek medical help for a chronic illness, the disease can deteriorate to a point where it is extremely difficult to control it.

The end stage of the kidney disease is kidney failure, which is otherwise termed End-stage Renal Disease or ESRD. At this period the kidneys no longer function, and the person can only survive on dialysis or by receiving a healthy kidney through transplant.

The Five Stages of Kidney Disease

Chronic kidney disease is categorized into five stages, each one characterized by a certain degree of damage done to the kidneys and rate of glomerular filtration, which is the rate at which filtration takes place in the kidneys. These help us understand just how well the kidneys are functioning.

Stage 1

The first stage is the least severe and actually comes close to a healthy state of your kidneys. Most people will never be aware if they have entered stage 1 of chronic kidney disease, or CKD. In many cases, if people discover stage 1 CKD, then it is because they were being tested for diabetes or high blood pressure. Otherwise, people can find out about stage 1 CKD if they discover protein or blood in the urine, signs of kidney damage in an ultrasound, a computerized tomography (CT) scan or through magnetic resonance imaging (MRI). If people have a family history of polycystic kidney disease (PKD), then there are chances that they might have CKD as well.

Stage 2

In this stage, there is a mild decrease in the glomerular filtration rate. People don't usually notice any symptoms at this stage as well. The reasons for discovering any signs of CKD are the same as with the reasons provided in stage 1.

So, what's the difference between stage 1 and stage 2? It all lies in the glomerular filtration rate, or GFR for short. The GFR is measured in milliliters/minute.

In stage 1, the glomerular filtration rate (GFR) is around 90 ml/min. The normal range of the GFR is from 90 ml/min to 120 ml/min. So, as you can see, stage 1 CKD shows a GFR at the lower end of the range. Because it falls so close to a normal rate, it easily goes unnoticed. At stage 2, the GFR falls to between 60-89 ml/min. You might become concerned with the range stage 2 falls in, but your kidneys are actually resilient. Even if they are not functioning at 100 percent, your kidneys are capable of doing a good job. So good that you might not notice anything was out of the ordinary.

Even though the differences between stage 1 and 2 are minuscule, they cannot be combined because the chances of someone showing certain symptoms of CKD when in stage 2 are greater.

Stage 3

At this stage, the kidneys suffer moderate damage. In order to properly gauge the level of damage, this stage is further divided into two: stage 3A and stage 3B. The reason for the division is because even though the severity of the disease worsens from 3A to 3B, the damage to the kidneys is still within moderate levels.

Each of the divisions are characterized by their GFR.

- 3A has a GFR between 45-59 ml/min

- 3B has a GFR between 30-44 ml/min

When patients reach stage 3, they begin to experience other symptoms of CKD, which include the below:

- Increase in fatigue

- Shortness of breath and swelling of extremities, also called edema Slight kidney pain, where the pain is felt in the lower back area Change in the color of urine

Stage 4

At stage 4, the kidney disease becomes severe. The GFR falls down to 15-30 ml/min. As the waste buildup increases the patient might experience nausea and vomiting, a buildup of urea in the blood that could cause bad breath, and find themselves having trouble doing everyday tasks such as reading a newspaper or trying to write up an email.

It is important to see a nephrologists' (a doctor who specializes in kidney problems) when the patient reaches stage 4.

Stage 5

At stage 5, the kidneys have a GFR of less than 15 ml/min. This is a truly low rate that causes the waste buildup to reach a critical point. The organs have reached an advanced stage CKD, causing them to lose almost all their abilities in order to function normally.

FOOD ALLOWED AND FOOD FORBIDDEN

Certain foods are generally good for health and specifically instrumental in mitigating kidney ailments. On the other hand, some foods that are otherwise fine can become a cause for kidney problems if taken in large quantities.

FOODS UNSUITABLE FOR KIDNEYS

Foods with potential to overload the kidneys should be avoided. In fact, foods that have been pre-packaged are discouraged as they usually have excess salt.

EXCESS SALTS & MINERALS

Sodium chloride, which is the ordinary salt used in the kitchen, should be taken in moderation. This is because not only is it bad for cases of diabetes, which is one of the diseases that aggravate kidney issues, but it can potentially reduce the capacity for the person to control the salt-water balance the body needs.

People need to understand that consuming too much salt contributes to incidences of high blood pressure, another health condition that aggravates kidney problems. The habit also causes fluids to accumulate in the body in an unhealthy way; and that becomes one major sign the kidneys are not functioning properly.

Consumption of foods rich in potassium and phosphorous should also be limited, because these minerals can lead to, or exacerbate kidney problems. Such foods include meat and dairy products, and even nuts.

When taken in moderate quantities, phosphorus plays its appropriate role of strengthening the bones. However, when taken in excess, it weakens the same bones while also causing damage to blood vessels, the heart and the eyes.

As for potassium, the body needs it for proper functioning of the nerves and the muscles, but if taken in excess it accumulates in the blood and ends up causing grave problems to the heart. It is important to remember that people with heart conditions are vulnerable to kidney disease as well.

Protein is another important nutrient but whose consumption should be kept moderate. If consumed in excess, protein can end up overworking the kidneys; hence leading to chronic kidney disease. Anyone with kidney issues needs to consult his/her doctor regarding the amount of protein to consume, and the right ratio of animal to plant protein.

UNSUITABLE FATS

It is crucial that people avoid inappropriate fats, which include trans fats and saturated fats. Trans fats are contained in oils that have been somewhat hydrogenated. They are fats present in foods such as frozen pizza, French fries and baked foodstuff like cakes and pies.

Saturated fats are present in certain foods even before processing. Examples of foods with saturated fats include red meat as well as dairy products. Between trans fats and saturated fats, trans fats are worse because not only do they raise the level of harmful cholesterol, but also lower the level of the healthy and helpful cholesterol.

FOODS BEST FOR THE KIDNEYS

When trying to avoid kidney problems through diet, it is recommended that people rely on home-made food rather than food bought from restaurants. In fact, if you have to buy such foods, check the label to confirm the sodium level does not go beyond 5%.

FRESH FOODS AND UNSATURATED FATS

The best foods for the sake of kidney health are those that are fresh. This is particularly so because they have no added salts and preservatives that might interfere with the functioning of the kidneys. Foods with unsaturated fats are also recommended for good health, and that includes the health of people with kidney issues. This category of fats includes those that are monounsaturated and those polyunsaturated.

01. Bulgur, Couscous, and Buckwheat Cereal

Preparation Time: 10 minutes

Cooking Time: 25 minutes

Servings: 4

Ingredients:

- ¼ cups Water
- ¼ cups Vanilla rice milk
- 6 Tbsps. Uncooked bulgur
- Tbsps. Uncooked whole buckwheat
- 1 cup Sliced apple
- 6 Tbsps. Plain uncooked couscous
- ½ tsp. Ground cinnamon

Directions:

1. Heat the water and milk in the saucepan over medium heat. Let it boil.
2. Put the bulgur, buckwheat, and apple.
3. Reduce the heat to low and simmer, occasionally stirring until the bulgur is tender, about 20 to 25 minutes.
4. Remove the saucepan and stir in the couscous and cinnamon— cover for 10 minutes.
5. Put the cereal before serving.

02. Buckwheat and Grapefruit Porridge

Preparation Time: 5 minutes

Cooking Time: 20 minutes

Servings: 2

Ingredients:

- ½ cup Buckwheat
- ¼ chopped Grapefruit
- 1 Tbsp. Honey
- 1 ½ cups Almond milk
- 2 cups Water

Directions:

1. Let the water boil on the stove. Add the buckwheat and place the lid on the pan.
2. Lower heat slightly and simmer for 7 to 10 minutes, checking to ensure water does not dry out.
3. When most of the water is absorbed, remove, and set aside for 5 minutes.
4. Drain any excess water from the pan and stir in almond milk, heating through for 5 minutes.
5. Add the honey and grapefruit.
6. Serve.

Nutrition: Calories: 231 Fat: 4g Carbs: 43g Protein: 13g Sodium: 135mg Potassium: 370mg Phosphorus: 165mg

03. Berry Chia with Yogurt

Preparation Time: 35 minutes

Cooking Time: 5 minutes

Servings:4

Ingredients:

- ½ cup chia seeds, dried
- 2 cup Plain yogurt
- 1/3 cup strawberries, chopped
- ¼ cup blackberries
- ¼ cup raspberries
- 4 teaspoons Splenda

Directions:

1. Mix up together Plain yogurt with Splenda, and chia seeds.
2. Transfer the mixture into the serving ramekins (jars) and leave for 35 minutes.
3. After this, add blackberries, raspberries, and strawberries. Mix up the meal well.
4. Serve it immediately or store it in the fridge for up to 2 days.

Nutrition: Calories: 150 Fat: 5g Carbs: 19g Protein: 6.8g Sodium: 65mg Potassium: 226mg Phosphorus: 75mg

04. Eggplant Chicken Sandwich

Preparation Time: 10 minutes

Cooking Time: 15 minutes

Servings: 2

Ingredients:

- 1 eggplant, trimmed
- 10 oz chicken fillet
- 1 teaspoon Plain yogurt
- ½ teaspoon minced garlic
- 2 tablespoon fresh cilantro, chopped
- lettuce leaves
- 1 teaspoon olive oil
- ½ teaspoon salt
- ½ teaspoon chili pepper
- 1 teaspoon butter

Directions:

1. Slice the eggplant lengthwise into 4 slices.
2. Rub the eggplant slices with minced garlic and brush with olive oil.
3. Grill the eggplant slices on the preheated to 375F grill for 3 minutes from each side.
4. Meanwhile, rub the chicken fillet with salt and chili pepper.

5. Place it in the skillet and add butter.

6. Roast the chicken for 6 minutes from each side over medium-high heat.

7. Cool the cooked eggplants gently and spread one side of them with Plain yogurt.

8. Add lettuce leaves and chopped fresh cilantro.

9. After this, slice the cooked chicken fillet and add over the lettuce.

10. Cover it with the remaining sliced eggplant to get the sandwich shape. Pin the sandwich with the toothpick if needed.

Nutrition: Calories: 276 Fat: 11g Carbs: 41g Protein: 13.8g Sodium: 775mg Potassium: 532mg Phosphorus: 187mg

05. Apple Pumpkin Muffins

Preparation time: 15 minutes

Cooking time: 20 minutes

Servings: 12

Ingredients

- 4 cup all-purpose flour

- 1 cup wheat bran

- 2 teaspoons phosphorus powder

- 1 cup pumpkin purée

- ¼ cup honey

- ¼ cup olive oil

- 1 egg

- 1 teaspoon vanilla extract

- ½ cup cored diced apple

Directions

1. Preheat the oven to 400°f.

2. Line 12 muffin cups with paper liners.

3. Stir together the flour, wheat bran, and baking powder, mix this in a medium bowl.

4. In a small bowl, whisk together the pumpkin, honey, olive oil, egg, and vanilla.

5. Stir the pumpkin mixture into the flour mixture until just combined.

6. Stir in the diced apple.

7. Spoon the batter in the muffin cups.

8. Bake for about 20 minutes, or until a toothpick inserted in the center of a muffin comes out clean.

Nutrition per serving: (1 muffin): calories: 125; total fat: 5g; saturated fat: 1g; cholesterol: 18mg; sodium: 8mg; carbohydrates: 20g; fiber: 3g; phosphorus: 120mg; potassium: 177mg; protein: 2g

06. Panzanella Salad

Preparation Time: 10 minutes

Cooking Time: 5 minutes

Servings: 4

Ingredients:

- 5 cucumbers, chopped
- 1 red onion, sliced
- red bell peppers, chopped
- ¼ cup fresh cilantro, chopped
- 1 tablespoon capers
- 1 oz whole-grain bread, chopped
- 1 tablespoon canola oil
- ½ teaspoon minced garlic
- 1 tablespoon Dijon mustard
- 1 teaspoon olive oil
- 1 teaspoon lime juice

Directions:

1. Pour canola oil into the skillet and bring it to boil.
2. Add chopped bread and roast it until crunchy (3-5 minutes).
3. Meanwhile, in the salad bowl, combinesliced red onion, cucumbers, bell peppers, cilantro, capers, and mix up gently.

4. Make the dressing: mix up together lime juice, olive oil, Dijon mustard, and minced garlic.

5. Put the dressing over the salad and stir it directly before serving.

Nutrition: Calories: 224.3 Fat: 10g Carbs: 26g Protein: 6.6g Sodium: 401mg Potassium: 324.9mg Phosphorus: 84mg

07. Pizza with Chicken and Pesto

Preparation Time: 10 minutes

Cooking Time: 25 minutes

Servings: 4

Ingredients:

- 1 ready-made frozen pizza dough
- 2/3 cup cooked chicken, chopped
- 1/2 cup of mango bell pepper, diced
- 1/2 cup of green bell pepper, diced
- 1/4 cup of purple onion, chopped
- 2 tbsp. of green basil pesto
- 1 tbsp. of chives, chopped
- 1/3 cup of parmesan or Romano cheese, grated
- 1/4 cup of mozzarella cheese
- 1 tbsp. of olive oil

Directions:

1. Thaw the pizza dough according to instructions on the package.

2. Heat the olive oil in a pan and sauté the peppers and onions for a couple of minutes. Set aside

3. Once the pizza dough has thawed, spread the Bali pesto over its surface.

4. Top with half of the cheese, the peppers, the onions, and the chicken. Finish with the rest of the cheese.

5. Bake at 350F/180C for approx. 20 minutes (or until crust and cheese are baked).

6. Slice in triangles with a pizza cutter or sharp knife and serve.

Nutrition: Calories: 225 Carbohydrate: 13.9 g Protein: 11.1 g Fat: 12 g Sodium: 321 mg Potassium: 174 mg Phosphorus: 172 mg

08. Marinated Shrimp Pasta Salad

Preparation Time: 15 minutes

Cooking Time: 5 hours

Servings: 1

Ingredients:

- 1/4 cup of honey

- 1/4 cup of balsamic vinegar

- 1/2 of an English cucumber, cubed

- 1/2 pound of fully cooked shrimp

- 15 baby carrots
- 1.5 cups of dime-sized cut cauliflower
- 4 stalks of celery, diced
- 1/2 large yellow bell pepper (diced)
- 1/2 red onion (diced)
- 1/2 large red bell pepper (diced)
- 12 ounces of uncooked tri-color pasta (cooked)
- 3/4 cup of olive oil
- 3 tsp. of mustard (Dijon)
- 1/2 tsp. of garlic (powder)
- 1/2 tsp. pepper

Directions:

1. Cut vegetables and put them in a bowl with the shrimp.

2. Whisk together the honey, balsamic vinegar, garlic powder, pepper, and Dijon mustard in a small bowl. While still whisking, slowly add the oil and whisk it all together.

3. Add the cooked pasta to the bowl with the shrimp and vegetables and mix it.

4. Toss the sauce to coat the pasta, shrimp, and vegetables evenly.

5. Cover and chill for a minimum of five hours before serving. Stir and serve while chilled.

Nutrition: Calories: 205 Fat: 13g Carbs: 10g Protein: 12g Sodium: 363mg Potassium: 156mg Phosphorus: 109mg

09. Peanut Butter and Jelly Grilled Sandwich

Preparation Time: 5 minutes

Cooking Time: 5 minutes

Servings: 1

Ingredients:

- 2 tsp. butter (unsalted)
- 6 tsp. butter (peanut)
- 3 tsp. of flavored jelly
- 2 pieces of bread

Directions:

1. Put the peanut butter evenly on one bread. Add the layer of jelly.
2. Butter the outside of the pieces of bread.
3. Add the sandwich to a frying pan and toast both sides.

Nutrition: Calories: 300 Fat: 7g Carbs: 49g Protein: 8g Sodium: 460mg Potassium: 222mg Phosphorus: 80mg

10. Grilled Onion and Pepper Jack Grilled Cheese Sandwich

Preparation Time: 5 minutes Cooking Time: 5 minutes Servings: 2

Ingredients:

- 1 tsp. of oil (olive)
- 6 tsp. of whipped cream cheese

- 1/2 of a medium onion
- 2 ounces of pepper jack cheese
- 4 slices of rye bread
- 2 tsp. of unsalted butter

Directions:

1. Set out the butter so that it becomes soft. Slice up the onion into thin slices.

2. Sauté onion slices. Continue to stir until cooked. Remove and put it to the side.

3. Spread one tablespoon of the whipped cream cheese on two of the slices of bread.

4. Then add grilled onions and cheese to each slice. Then top using the other two bread slices.

5. Spread the softened butter on the outside of the slices of bread.

6. Use the skillet to toast the sandwiches until lightly brown and the cheese is melted.

Nutrition: Calories: 350 Fat: 18g Carbs: 34g Protein: 13g Sodium: 589mg Potassium: 184mg Phosphorus: 226mg

11. Aromatic Carrot Cream

Preparation Time: 15 minutes

Cooking Time: 25 minutes

Servings: 4

Ingredients:

- 2 tablespoon olive oil
- ½ sweet onion, chopped
- 1 teaspoons fresh ginger, peeled and grated
- 1 teaspoon fresh garlic, minced
- 1 cups water
- 2 carrots, chopped
- 1 teaspoon ground turmeric
- ½ cup coconut almond milk

Directions:

1. Heat the olive oil into a big pan over medium-high heat.
2. Add the onion, garlic and ginger. Softly cook for about 3 minutes until softened.
3. Include the water, turmeric and the carrots. Softly cook for about 20 minutes (until the carrots are softened).
4. Blend the soup adding coconut almond milk until creamy.

Nutrition: Calories 112 Fat 10 g Cholesterol 0 mg Carbohydrates 8 g Sugar 5 g Fiber 2 g Protein 2 g Sodium 35 mg Calcium 32 mg Phosphorus 59 mg Potassium 241 mg

12. Mushrooms Velvet Soup

Preparation Time: 40 minutes

Cooking Time: 40 minutes

Servings: 6

Ingredients:

- 1 teaspoon olive oil
- ½ teaspoon fresh ground black pepper
- 3 medium (85g) shallots, diced
- 2 stalks (80g) celery, chopped
- 1 clove garlic, diced
- 12-ounces cremini mushrooms, sliced
- 5 tablespoons flour
- 4 cups low sodium vegetable stock, divided
- 3 sprigs fresh thyme
- 2 bay leaves
- ½ cup regular yogurt

Directions:

1. Heat oil in a large pan.
2. Add ground pepper, shallots and celery. Cook over medium-high heat.
3. Sauté for 2 minutes until golden.
4. Add garlic and stir.

5. Include the sliced mushrooms. Stir and cook until the mushrooms give out their liquid.

6. Sprawl the flour on the mushrooms and toast for about 2 min.

7. Add one cup of hot stock, thyme sprigs and bay leaves. Stir and add the second cup of stock

8. Stir until well combined.

9. Add the remaining cups of stock.

10. Slowly cook for 15 minutes.

11. Take out bay leaves and thyme sprigs.

12. Blend until mixture is smooth.

13. Include the yogurt and stir well.

14. Slowly cook for 4 minutes.

Nutrition: Calories 126 Fat 8 g Cholesterol 0 mg Carbohydrate 14 g Sugar 4 g Fiber 2 g Protein 3 g Sodium 108 mg Calcium 55 mg Phosphorus 70 mg Potassium 298 mg

13. Pumpkin Bites

Preparation Time: 10 minutes

Cooking Time: 5 minutes

Servings: 12

Ingredients:

- 8 oz cream cheese

- 1 tsp vanilla

- 1 tsp pumpkin pie spice

- 1/4 cup coconut flour

- 1/4 cup erythritol

- 1/2 cup pumpkin puree

- 4 oz butter

Directions:

1. Add all ingredients into the mixing bowl and beat using hand mixer until well combined.

2. Scoop mixture into the silicone ice cube tray and place it in the refrigerator until set.

3. Serve and enjoy.

Nutrition: Calories 149 Fat 14.6 g Carbohydrates 8.1 g Sugar 5.4 g Protein 2 g Cholesterol 41 mg Phosphorus: 66mg Potassium: 77mg Sodium: 55mg

14. Exotic Palabok

Preparation Time: 25 minutes

Cooking Time: 15 minutes

Servings: 6

Ingredients:

- 12 oz. rice noodles.

- 1 ½ cups of medium shrimp, peeled and deveined

- 2/3 cup of white onion, chopped

- 1 spring onion, sliced

- 3 tbsp. of canola oil

- 1-pound, lean ground turkey

- 2 cups of firm tofu, chopped

- 2 packs of shrimp or ordinary gravy mix

- 5 hard-boiled eggs

- 1 lemon

- ½ cup of pork rinds (optional)

Directions:

1. Boil rice noodles until nice and soft. Keep aside.

2. Boil the peeled shrimp for 2-3 minutes in a pot with plain water.

3. In a wok or shallow pan, sauté the garlic and onion with the oil. Add the ground turkey, tofu, and shrimps.

4. Dissolve the gravy mix in water or as per package instructions.

5. Combine the rice noodles, tofu, onions, and the gravy mix with ½ cup of pork rind (optional).

6. Slice the egg and lemons.

7. Serve with egg and lemons on top.

Nutrition: Calories: 305 kcal Carbohydrate: 39.14g Protein: 17.6g Sodium: 536mg Potassium: 243.52 mg Phosphorus: 180.41mg Dietary Fiber: 0.9g

15. Marinated Shrimp and Pasta

Preparation Time: 10 minutes

Cooking Time: 20 minutes

Servings: 10

Ingredients:

- 12 oz. of three-colored penne pasta
- ½ pound of cooked shrimp
- ½ red bell pepper, diced
- ½ cup of red onion, chopped 3 stalks of celery
- 12 baby carrots, cut into thick slices
- 1 cup of cauliflower, cut into small round pieces
- ¼ cup of honey
- ¼ cup balsamic vinegar
- ½ tsp. of black pepper
- ½ tsp. garlic powder
- 1 tbsp. of French mustard
- ¾ cup of olive oil

Directions:

1. Cook pasta for around 10 minutes (or according to packaged instructions).

2. While pasta is boiling, cut all your veggies and place into a large mixing bowl. Add the cooked shrimp.

3. In a mixing bowl, add the honey, vinegar, black pepper, garlic powder, and mustard. While you whisk, slowly incorporate the oil and stir well.

4. Add in the drained pasta with the veggies and shrimp and gently combine everything. Pour the liquid marinade over the pasta and veggies and toss to coat everything evenly.

5. Refrigerate for 3-5 hours before serving. Serve chilled.

Nutrition: Calories: 256kcal Carbohydrate: 41g Protein: 6.55g Sodium: 242.04mg Potassium: 131.88mg Phosphorus: 86.03mg Dietary Fiber: 2.28g Fat: 16.88g

16. Steak and Onion Sandwich

Preparation Time: 25 minutes

ooking Time: 8 minutes

Servings: 4

Ingredients:

- 4 flank steaks (around 4 oz. each)

- 1 medium red onion, sliced

- 1 tbsp. of lemon juice

- 1 tbsp. of Italian seasoning

- 1 tsp. of black pepper

- 1 tbsp. of vegetable oil

- 4 sandwich/burger buns

Directions:

1. Wrap the steak with the lemon juice, the Italian seasoning, and pepper to taste. Cut into 4 pieces Heat the vegetable oil in a medium skillet over medium heat.

2. Cook steaks around 3 minutes on each side until you get a medium to well-done result. Take off and transfer onto a dish with absorbing paper.

3. In the same skillet, sauté the onions until tender and transparent (around 3 minutes).

4. Cut the sandwich bun into half and place 1 piece of steak in each topped with the onions. Serve or wrap with paper or foil and keep in the fridge for the next day.

Nutrition: Calories: 315.26 kcal Carbohydrate: 8.47g Protein: 38.33g Sodium: 266.24mg Potassium: 238.2mg

Phosphorus: 364.25mg Dietary Fiber: 0.76g Fat: 13.22g

17. Crab Cakes

Preparation Time: 25 minutes Cooking Time: 6 minutes Servings: 6

Ingredients:

- 9 oz. (250 grams) of crab meat

- 1/3 cup of green or red bell pepper, thinly chopped

- 1/3 cup of low salt crackers, crushed

- ¼ cup of low-fat mayonnaise

- 1 tbsp. of dry mustard

- ½ tsp. of pepper

- 2 tbsp. of lemon juice

- ½ tsp. of lemon zest

- 1 tsp. of garlic powder 2 tbsp. of vegetable oil

Directions:

1. Mix all the ingredients except for the oil until uniform. Divide into 6 flat patties (around 5 inches in diameter).

2. Heat the vegetable oil in the skillet and shallow fry the patties for 2-3 minutes on each side (or until golden brown).

3. Serve warm on a dish with absorbing paper.

Nutrition: Calories: 144.42kcal Carbohydrate: 5.12g Protein: 8.47g Sodium: 212.31mg Potassium: 195mg Phosphorus: 127.42mg Dietary Fiber: 1.02g Fat: 9.2g

18. Zucchini Noodles with Spring Vegetables

Preparation Time: 20 minutes

Cooking Time: 10 minutes

Servings: 6

Ingredients:

- 6 zucchinis, cut into long noodles

- 1 cup of halved snow peas

- 1 cup (3-inch pieces) of asparagus

- 1 tablespoon of olive oil

- 1 teaspoon of minced fresh garlic

- 1 tablespoon of freshly squeezed lemon juice

- 2 tablespoons of chopped fresh basil leaves

Directions:

1. Fill a medium saucepan with water, place over medium-high heat, and bring to a boil.

2. Reduce the heat to medium, and blanch the zucchini ribbons, snow peas, and asparagus by submerging them in the water for 1 minute. Drain and rinse immediately under cold water.

3. Pat the vegetables dry with paper towels, and transfer to a large bowl.

4. Place a medium skillet over medium heat, and add the olive oil. Add the garlic, and sauté until tender, about 3 minutes.

5. Add the lemon juice

6. Add the zucchini mixture, and basil and toss until well combined.

7. Serve immediately.

Nutrition: Calories: 52 Total fat: 2g Saturated fat: 0g Cholesterol: 0mg Sodium: 7mg Carbohydrates: 4g Fiber: 1g Phosphorus: 40mg Potassium: 197mg Protein: 2g

19. Asparagus Lime Spaghetti

Preparation Time: 5 minutes

Cooking Time: 20 minutes

Servings: 6

Ingredients:

- 1 pound of asparagus spears, trimmed and cut into
- 2-inch pieces 2 teaspoons of olive oil
- 2 teaspoons of minced garlic
- 2 teaspoons of all-purpose flour
- 1 cup of Homemade Rice Almond milk (here, or use unsweetened store-bought) or almond milk
- Juice and zest of ½ lemon
- 1 tablespoon of chopped fresh thyme Freshly ground black pepper
- 2 cups of cooked spaghetti
- ¼ cup of grated Parmesan cheese

Directions:

1. Fill a large saucepan with water and bring to a boil over high heat. Add the asparagus and blanch until crisp-tender, about 2 minutes. Drain and set aside.

2. In a large skillet over medium-high heat, heat the olive oil. Add the garlic, and sauté until softened, about 2 minutes. Whisk in the flour to create a paste, about 1 minute. Whisk in the rice almond milk, lemon juice, lemon zest, and thyme.

3. Reduce the heat to medium and cook the sauce, whisking constantly, until thickened and creamy, about 3 minutes.

4. Season the sauce with pepper.

5. Stir in the spaghetti and the asparagus.

6. Serve the pasta topped with the Parmesan cheese.

Nutrition: Calories:127 Total fat: 3g Saturated fat: 1g Cholesterol: 4mg Sodium: 67mg Carbohydrates: 19g

Fiber: 2g Phosphorus 109mg Potassium: 200mg Protein: 6g

20. Spicy Cabbage Dish

Preparation Time: 10 minutes

Cooking Time: 4 hours

Servings: 4

Ingredients:

- 1 yellow onions, chopped
- 10 cups red cabbage, shredded
- 1 cup plums, pitted and chopped
- 1 teaspoon cinnamon powder
- 1 garlic clove, minced
- 1 teaspoon cumin seeds
- ¼ teaspoon cloves, ground
- 2 tablespoons red wine vinegar
- 1 teaspoon coriander seeds
- ½ cup water

Directions:

4. Add cabbage, onion, plums, garlic, cumin, cinnamon, cloves, vinegar, coriander and water to your Slow Cooker.

5. Stir well.

6. Place lid and cook on LOW for 4 hours.

7. Divide between serving platters.

Nutrition: Calories: 197 Fat: 1g Carbohydrates: 14g Protein: 3g Phosphorus: 115mg Potassium: 119mg Sodium: 75mg

21. Extreme Balsamic Chicken

Preparation Time: 10 minutes

Cooking Time: 35 minutes

Servings: 4

Ingredients:

- 3 boneless chicken breasts, skinless Sunflower seeds to taste

- ¼ cup almond flour

- 2/3 cups low-fat chicken broth

- 1 ½ teaspoons arrowroot

- ½ cup low sugar raspberry preserve

- 1 ½ tablespoons balsamic vinegar

Directions:

1. Cut chicken breast into bite-sized pieces and season them with seeds.

2. Dredge the chicken pieces in flour and shake off any excess.

3. Take a non-stick skillet and place it over medium heat.

4. Add chicken to the skillet and cook for 15 minutes, making sure to turn them half-way through.

5. Remove chicken and transfer to platter.

6. Add arrowroot, broth, raspberry preserve to the skillet and stir.

7. Stir in balsamic vinegar and reduce heat to low, stir-cook for a few minutes.

8. Transfer the chicken back to the sauce and cook for 15 minutes more.

9. Serve and enjoy!

Nutrition: Calories: 546 Fat: 35g Carbohydrates: 11g Protein: 44g Phosphorus: 120mg Potassium: 117mg Sodium: 85mg

22. Enjoyable Green lettuce and Bean Medley

Servings: 4

Preparation Time: 10 minutes

Cooking Time: 4 hours

Ingredients:

- 5 carrots, sliced

- 1 ½ cups great northern beans, dried

- 2 garlic cloves, minced

- 1 yellow onion, chopped Pepper to taste

- ½ teaspoon oregano, dried

- 5 ounces baby green lettuce

- 4 ½ cups low sodium veggie stock

- 2 teaspoons lemon peel, grated

- 3 tablespoon lemon juice

Directions:

1. Add beans, onion, carrots, garlic, oregano and stock to your Slow Cooker.

2. Stir well.

3. Place lid and cook on HIGH for 4 hours.

4. Add green lettuce, lemon juice and lemon peel.

5. Stir and let it sit for 5 minutes.

6. Divide between serving platters and enjoy!

Nutrition: Calories: 219 Fat: 8g Carbohydrates: 14g Protein: 8g Phosphorus: 210mg Potassium: 217mg Sodium: 85mg

23. Tantalizing Cauliflower and Dill Mash

Preparation Time: 10 minutes

Cooking Time: 6 hours

Servings: 6

Ingredients:

- 1 cauliflower head, florets separated

- 1/3 cup dill, chopped

- 6 garlic cloves

- 2 tablespoons olive oil Pinch of black pepper

Directions:

1. Add cauliflower to Slow Cooker.

2. Add dill, garlic and water to cover them.

3. Place lid and cook on HIGH for 5 hours.

4. Drain the flowers.

5. Season with pepper and add oil, mash using potato masher.

6. Whisk and serve.

7. Enjoy!

Nutrition: Calories: 207 Fat: 4g Carbohydrates: 14g Protein: 3g Phosphorus: 130mg Potassium: 107mg Sodium: 105mg

24. Green Tuna Salad

Preparation Time: 10 minutes

Cooking Time: 15 -20 minutes

Servings: 2

Ingredients:

- 5 ounces of tuna (in freshwater only)

- 2-3 cups of lettuce

- 1 cup of baby marrows

- 1/2 cup of red bell pepper

- 1/4 cup of red onion

- 1/4 cup of fresh thyme

- 2 tbsp olive oil

- 1/8 tsp of black pepper

- 2 tbsp of red wine vinegar

Directions:

1. Chop the bell pepper, onion, baby marrow, and thyme into small pieces.

2. Add a 3/4 cup of water to a saucepan and add the bell pepper, onion, baby marrow, and thyme to the pan. Let it boil, steam the vegetables by adding a lid on top of the saucepan—steam for 10 minutes.

3. Remove the vegetables and drain them.

4. Combine the vegetables (once cooled down) with the chopped tuna.

5. Mix olive oil, red wine vinegar, and black pepper to create a salad dressing.

6. Add the mixture on a bed of lettuce and drizzle the dressing on top.

Nutrition: Calories: 210 Fat: 1.5g Carbs: 4g Protein: 43.3g Sodium: 726mg Potassium: 582mg Phosphorus: 296mg

25. Roasted Chicken and Vegetables

Preparation Time: 10 minutes

Cooking Time: 45 minutes

Servings: 2

Ingredients:

- 8 oz chicken strips
- 5 oz green beans
- 2 tbsp sesame seed oil
- 1 tsp of Cajun chicken spice
- ½ tbsp Italian herb dressing

Directions:

1. Heat the oven to 400 degrees-Fahrenheit
2. Fill up a large pot with water until it is ¾ full.
3. Chop off the tips of the green beans.
4. Line a 9 x 13-inch oven tray with parchment paper or spray the oven tray with cooking spray.
5. Place the chicken strips on the tray side, with the green beans
6. Add Cajun chicken spice to the chicken breasts and drizzle sesame seed oil over the chicken and vegetables.
7. Roast for 20 minutes.
8. Drizzle Italian herb dressing on top of the chicken and vegetables and roast for another 5-10 minutes.

Nutrition: Calories: 263 Fat: 6g Sodium: 366mg Potassium: 879mg Phosphorus: 275mg Carbs: 28.6g Protein: 23g

26. Chinese Beef Wraps

Preparation Time: 10 minutes

Cooking Time: 30 minutes

Servings: 2

Ingredients:

- 1iceberg lettuce leaves

- ½ diced cucumber

- 1 teaspoon canola oil

- 5-ounce lean ground beef

- 1 teaspoon ground ginger

- 1 tablespoon chili flakes

- 1 minced garlic clove

- 1 tablespoon rice wine vinegar

Directions:

1. Mix the ground meat with the garlic, rice wine vinegar, chili flakes, and ginger in a bowl. Heat-up oil in a skillet over medium heat.

2. Put the beef in the pan and cook for 20-25 minutes or until cooked through. Serve beef mixture with diced cucumber in each lettuce wrap and fold.

Nutrition: Calories 156 Fat 2g Carbs 4 g Phosphorus 1 mg Sodium 54mg Protein 14g Potassium 0mg

27. Spicy Lamb Curry

Preparation Time: 15 minutes

Cooking Time: 2 hours 15 minutes

Servings: 6-8

Ingredients:

- 4 teaspoons ground coriander
- 4 teaspoons ground coriander
- 4 teaspoons ground cumin
- ¾ teaspoon ground ginger
- 2 teaspoons ground cinnamon
- ½ teaspoon ground cloves
- ½ teaspoon ground cardamom
- 2 tablespoons sweet paprika
- ½ tablespoon cayenne pepper
- 2 teaspoons chili powder
- 2 teaspoons salt
- 1 tablespoon coconut oil
- 2pounds boneless lamb, trimmed and cubed into 1-inch size
- Salt ground black pepper
- 2 cups onions, chopped
- 1¼ cups water
- 1 cup of coconut almond milk

Directions:

1. For spice mixture in a bowl, mix all spices. Keep aside. Season the lamb with salt and black pepper.

2. Warm oil on medium-high heat in a large Dutch oven. Add lamb and stir fry for around 5 minutes. Add onion and cook approximately 4-5 minutes.

3. Stir in the spice mixture and cook approximately 1 minute. Add water and coconut almond milk and provide some boil on high heat.

4. Adjust the heat to low and simmer, covered for approximately 1- 120 minutes or until the lamb's desired doneness. Uncover and simmer for about 3-4 minutes. Serve hot.

Nutrition: Calories: 466 Fat: 10g Carbohydrates: 23g Protein: 36g Potassium 599 mg Sodium 203 mg Phosphorus 0mg

28. Roast Beef

Preparation Time: 25 minutes Cooking Time: 55 minutes Servings: 3

Ingredients:

- Quality rump or sirloin tip roast Pepper & herbs

Directions:

1. Place in a roasting pan on a shallow rack. Season with pepper and herbs. Insert meat thermometer in the center or thickest part of the roast.

2. Roast to the desired degree of doneness. After removing from over for about 15 minutes, let it chill. In the end, the roast should be moister than well done.

Nutrition: Calories 158 Protein 24 g Fat 6 g Carbs 0 g Phosphorus 206 mg Potassium 328 mg Sodium 55 mg

29. Lemon and Thyme Lamb Chops

Preparation time: 10 min

Cooking Time: 10 minutes

Servings: 4

Ingredients:

- 1 tablespoon olive oil

- 1/4 tablespoon lemon juice

- 1 tablespoon chopped fresh thyme

- Salt and pepper to taste

- 4 lamb chops

Directions:

1. Stir together olive oil, lemon juice, and thyme in a small bowl. Season with salt and pepper to taste. Place lamb chops in a shallow dish and brush with the olive oil mixture. Marinate in the refrigerator for 1 hour.

2. Preheat grill for high heat.

3. Lightly oil grill grate. Place lamb chops on the grill, and discard marinade. Cook for 10 minutes, turning once, or to the desired doneness

Nutrition: Calories 111, Total Fat 6.7g, Saturated Fat 1.6g, Cholesterol 38mg, Sodium 33mg, Total Carbohydrate 0.5g, Dietary Fiber 0.3g, Total Sugars 0g, Protein 12g, Calcium 19mg, Iron 2mg, Potassium 149mg, Phosphorus 93mg

30. Basil Grilled Mediterranean Lamb Chops

Preparation time: 10 min

Cooking Time: 10 minutes

Servings: 4

Ingredients:

- 4 (8 ounces) lamb shoulder chops
- 2 tablespoons Dijon mustard
- 3 tablespoons balsamic vinegar
- ½ tablespoon garlic powder
- 1/4 teaspoon ground black pepper
- 1/2 cup olive oil
- 2 tablespoons shredded fresh basil, or to taste

Directions:

1. Pat lamb chops dry and arrange in a single layer in a shallow glass baking dish.

2. Whisk Dijon mustard, balsamic vinegar, garlic, and pepper together in a small bowl.

3. Whisk in oil slowly until marinade is smooth.

4. Stir in basil. Pour marinade over lamb chops, turning to coat both sides.

5. Cover and refrigerate for 1 to 4 hours.

6. Bring lamb chops to room temperature, about 30 minutes.

7. Preheat grill for medium heat and lightly oil the grate.

8. Grill lamb chops until browned, 5 to 10 minutes per side.

9. An instant-read thermometer inserted into the center should read at least 145 degrees F.

Nutrition: Calories 270, Total Fat 27.8g, Saturated Fat 4.4g, Cholesterol 19mg, Sodium 109mg, Total Carbohydrate 1.4g, Dietary Fiber 0.4g, Total Sugars 0.4g, Protein 6.1g, Calcium 14mg, Iron 1mg, Potassium 33mg, Phosphorus 30mg

31. Curry Lamb Balls

Preparation Time: 15 minutes

Cooking Time: 7 hours

Servings: 6

Ingredients:

- 1/2 medium red onion, sliced thinly

- 1/2 tablespoon vegetable oil

- 10ounce of flat-cut beef brisket, whole

- ½ cup low sodium stock

- ¾ cup of water

- ½ tablespoon honey

- ½ tablespoon chili powder

- ½ teaspoon smoked paprika

- ½ teaspoon dried thyme

- 1 teaspoon black pepper

- 1 tablespoon corn starch

Directions:

1. Throw the sliced onion into the slow cooker first. Add a splash of oil to a large hot skillet and briefly seal the beef on all sides.

2. Remove the beef, then place it in the slow cooker. Add the stock, water, honey, and spices to the same skillet you cooked the beef meat.

3. Allow the juice to simmer until the volume is reduced by about half. Pour the juice over beef in the slow cooker. Cook on low within 7 hours.

4. Transfer the beef to your platter, shred it using two forks. Put the rest of the juice into a medium saucepan. Bring it to a simmer.

5. Whisk the cornstarch with two tablespoons of water. Add to the juice and cook until slightly thickened.

6. For a thicker sauce, simmer and reduce the juice a bit more before adding cornstarch. Put the sauce on the meat and serve.

Nutrition: Calories: 128 Protein: 13g Carbohydrates: 6g Fat: 6g Sodium: 228mg Potassium: 202mg Phosphorus: 119mg

32. Chunky Beef Slow Roast

Preparation Time: 15 minutes

Cooking Time: 5-6 hours

Servings: 12

Ingredients:

- 2 cups of peeled carrots, chunked
- 1 cup of onion
- 2 garlic cloves, chopped
- 1 ¼ pound flat-cut beef brisket, fat trimmed
- 2 cups of water
- 1 teaspoon of chili powder
- 1 tablespoon of dried rosemary

- For the sauce:
- 1 tablespoon of freshly grated horseradish
- ½ cup of almond milk (unenriched)
- 1 tablespoon lemon juice (freshly squeezed)
- 1 garlic clove, minced
- A pinch of cayenne pepper

Directions:

1. Double boil the carrots to reduce their potassium content. Chop the onion and the garlic. Place the beef brisket in a slow cooker.

2. Combine water, chopped garlic, chili powder, and rosemary.

3. Pour the mixture over the brisket. Cover and cook on high within 4- 5 hours until the meat is very tender. Drain the carrots and add them to the slow cooker.

4. Adjust the heat to high and cook covered until the carrots are tender. Prepare the horseradish sauce by whisking together horseradish, almond milk, lemon juice, minced garlic, and cayenne pepper.

5. Cover and refrigerate. Serve your casserole with a dash of horseradish sauce on the side.

Nutrition: Calories: 199 Protein: 21g Carbohydrates: 12g Fat: 7g Sodium: 282mg Potassium: 317 Phosphorus: 191mg

33. Beef Ragu

Preparation Time: 10 minutes

Cooking Time: 10 minutes

Servings: 2

Ingredients:

- 1/4 cup packaged pesto
- 1 teaspoon salt
- 2 large zucchinis, cut into noodle strips
- 1 tablespoon olive oil
- 1/4-pound ground beef
- 4 tablespoons fresh parsley, chopped

Directions:

1. Heat the oil in a skillet under medium flame and cook the ground beef until thoroughly cooked, around 5 minutes. Discard excess fat.

2. Add the packaged pesto sauce and season with salt. Add
   t

3. Then chopped parsley and cook for three more minutes.
   Set aside.

4. In the same saucepan, place the zucchini noodles and
   cook for five minutes. Turn off the heat then add the
   cooked meat. Mix well.

5. Serve and enjoy.

Nutrition:

Calories 353, Total Fat 30g, Saturated Fat 6g, Total Carbs 2g,
Net Carbs 1.3g, Protein 19g, Sugar: 0.3g, Fiber 0.7g, Sodium
1481mg, Potassium 341mg

34. Open-Faced Beef Stir-Up

Preparation Time: 10 minutes

Cooking Time: 10 minutes

Servings: 6

Ingredients:

- 95% Lean ground beef –

- 1/2 pound Chopped sweet onion

- 1/2 cup Shredded cabbage

- 1/2 cup Herb pesto

- 1/4 cup Hamburger buns

- 6, bottom halves only

Directions:

1. Sauté the beef and onion for 6 minutes or until beef is cooked.

2. Add the cabbage and sauté for 3 minutes more.

3. Stir in pesto and heat for 1 minute.

4. Divide the beef mixture into 6 portions and serve each on the bottom half of a hamburger bun, open-face.

Nutrition: **Calories:** 120 Fat: 3g Phosphorus: 106mg Potassium: 198mg Sodium: 134mg Protein: 11g

35. Homemade Burgers

Preparation Time: 10 minutes

Cooking Time: 20 minutes

Servings: 2

Ingredients:

- 4 ounce lean 100% ground beef
- 1 teaspoon black pepper
- 1 garlic clove, minced
- 1 teaspoon olive oil
- 1/4 cup onion, finely diced
- 1 tablespoon balsamic vinegar
- 1/2ounce brie cheese, crumbled
- 1 teaspoon mustard

Directions:

1. Season ground beef with pepper and then mix in minced garlic.

2. Form burger shapes with the ground beef using the palms of your hands.

3. Heat a skillet on a medium to high heat, and then add the oil.

4. Sauté the onions for 5-10 minutes until browned.

5. Then add the balsamic vinegar and sauté for another 5 minutes.

6. Remove and set aside.

7. Add the burgers to the pan and heat on the same heat for 5-6 minutes before flipping and heating for a further 5-6 minutes until cooked through.

8. Spread the mustard onto each burger.

9. Crumble the brie cheese over each burger and serve!

10. Try with a crunchy side salad!

Tip: If using fresh beef and not defrosted, prepare double the ingredients and freeze burgers in plastic wrap (after cooling) for up to 1 month.

Thoroughly defrost before heating through completely in the oven to serve.

Nutrition: Calories: 178 Fat: 10g Carbohydrates: 4g Phosphorus: 147mg Potassium: 272mg Sodium: 273 mg Protein: 16g

36. Fruity Chicken Salad

Preparation Time: 10 minutes

Cooking Time: 5 minutes

Servings: 3

Ingredients:

- 4 skinless, boneless chicken breast halves - cooked and diced
- 1 stalk celery, diced
- 4 green onions, chopped
- 1Golden Delicious apple - peeled, cored and diced
- 1/3 cup seedless green grapes, halved
- 1/8 teaspoon ground black pepper
- 3/4 cup light mayonnaise

Directions:

1. In a large container, add the celery, chicken, onion, apple, grapes, pepper, and mayonnaise.
2. Mix all together. Serve!

Nutrition: Calories 196, Sodium 181mg, Total Carbohydrate 15.6g, Dietary Fiber 1.2g, Total Sugars 9.1g, Protein 13.2g, Calcium 13mg, Iron 1mg, Potassium 115mg, Phosphorus 88 mg

37. Buckwheat Salad

Preparation Time: 12 minutes

Cooking Time: 20 minutes

Servings: 3

Ingredients:

- 2 cups water
- 1 clove garlic, smashed
- 1 cup uncooked buckwheat
- 2 large cooked chicken breasts - cut into bite-size pieces
  1 large red onion, diced
- 1 large green bell pepper, diced
- 1/4 cup chopped fresh parsley
- 1/4 cup chopped fresh chives
- 1/2 teaspoon salt
- 2/3 cup fresh lemon juice
- 1 tablespoon balsamic vinegar
- 1/4 cup olive oil

Directions:

1. Bring the water, garlic to a boil in a saucepan. Stir in the buckwheat, reduce heat to medium-low, cover, and simmer until the buckwheat is tender and the water has been absorbed, 15 to 20 minutes.

2. Discard the garlic clove and scrape the buckwheat into a large bowl.

3. Gently stir the chicken, onion, bell pepper, parsley, chives, and salt into the buckwheat.

4. Sprinkle with the olive oil, balsamic vinegar, and lemon juice. Stir until evenly mixed.

Nutrition: Calories 199, Total Fat 8.3g, Sodium 108mg, Dietary Fiber 2.9g, Total Sugars 2g, Protein 13.6g, Calcium 22mg, Potassium 262mg, Phosphorus 188 mg

38. Oven-Baked Turkey Thighs

Preparation Time: 10 minutes

Cooking Time: 30 minutes

Servings: 4

Ingredients:

- 10 ounces turkey thighs, skin on, bone-in
- 1/3 cup white wine
- 1 lemon
- 1 tablespoon fresh oregano
- 1/4 teaspoon cracked black pepper
- 1 tablespoon olive oil

Directions:

1. Heat the oven to 350 degrees F.

2. Add turkey thighs and white wine to an oven-proof pan. Squeeze half the lemon over turkey. Slice remaining lemon and top turkey with lemon slices.

3. Season turkey with fresh oregano, cracked pepper and olive oil.

4. Bake turkey for 25 to 30 minutes or until internal temperature reaches 165 degrees F to 175 degrees F.

Nutrition: Calories 189, Sodium 62mg, Dietary Fiber 0.9g, Total Sugars 0.6g, Protein 20.8g, Calcium 34mg, Potassium 232mg, Phosphorus 180 mg

39. Southern Fried Chicken

Preparation Time: 5 minutes

Cooking Time: 26 minutes

Servings: 2

Ingredients:

- 2 x 6-oz. boneless skinless chicken breasts
- 2 tbsp. hot sauce
- ½ tsp. onion powder
- 1 tbsp. chili powder
- 2oz. pork rinds, finely ground

Directions:

1. Chop the chicken breasts in half lengthways and rub in the hot sauce. Combine the onion powder with the chili powder, then rub into the chicken. Leave to marinate for at least a half hour.

2. Use the ground pork rinds to coat the chicken breasts in the ground pork rinds, covering them thoroughly. Place the chicken in your fryer.

3. Set the fryer at 350°F and cook the chicken for 13 minutes. Turn over the chicken and cook the other side for another 13 minutes or until golden.

4. Test the chicken with a meat thermometer. When fully cooked, it should reach 165°F. Serve hot, with the sides of your choice.

Nutrition: Calories: 408 Fat: 19 g Carbs: 10 g Protein: 35 g Calcium 39mg, Phosphorous 216mg, Potassium 137mg Sodium: 153 mg

40. Basil Chicken over Macaroni

Preparation Time: 10 minutes

Cooking Time: 30 minutes

Servings: 4

Ingredients:

- 1 (8 ounces) package macaroni

- 2 teaspoons olive oil

- 1/2 cup finely chopped onion

- 1 clove garlic, chopped

- 2 cups boneless chicken breast halves, cooked and cubed

- 1/4 cup chopped fresh basil

- 1/4 cup Parmesan cheese

- 1/2 teaspoon black pepper

Directions:

1. In a large pot of boiling water, cook macaroni until it is al dente, about 8 to 10 minutes. Drain, and set aside.

2. In a large skillet, heat oil over medium-high heat. Sauté the onions and garlic. Stir in the chicken, basil, and pepper.

3. Reduce heat to medium, and cover skillet. Simmer for about 5 minutes, stirring frequently,

4. Toss sauce with hot cooked macaroni to coat. Serve with Parmesan cheese.

Nutrition: Calories 349, Sodium 65mg, Dietary Fiber 2.2g, Total Sugars 2.1g, Protein 28.5g, Calcium 44mg, Potassium 286mg, Phosphorus 280 mg

41. Roasted Citrus Chicken

Preparation Time: 20 Minutes

Cooking Time: 60 Minutes

Servings: 8

Ingredients:

- 1 tablespoon olive oil

- 2 cloves garlic, minced

- 1 teaspoon Italian seasoning

- 1/2 teaspoon black pepper

- 8 chicken thighs

- 2 cups chicken broth, reduced sodium

- 3 tablespoons lemon juice

- 1/2 large chicken breast for 1 chicken thigh

Directions:

1. Warm oil in a huge skillet.

2. Include garlic and seasonings.

3. Include chicken bosoms and dark-colored all sides.

4. Spot chicken in the moderate cooker and include the chicken soup.

5. Cook on LOW heat for 6 to 8 hours

6. Include lemon juice toward the part of the bargain time.

Nutrition: Calories 265, Fat 19g, Protein 21g, Carbohydrates 1g

42. Chicken with Asian Vegetables

Preparation Time: 10 Minutes

Cooking Time: 20 Minutes

Servings: 8

Ingredients:

- 2 tablespoons canola oil

- 6 boneless chicken breasts

- 1 cup low-sodium chicken broth

- 3 tablespoons reduced-sodium soy sauce

- 1/4 teaspoon crushed red pepper flakes

- 1 garlic clove, crushed

- 1 can (8ounces) water chestnuts, sliced and rinsed (optional)
- 1/2 cup sliced green onions
- 1 cup chopped red or green bell pepper
- 1 cup chopped celery
- 1/4 cup cornstarch
- 1/3 cup water
- 3 cups cooked white rice
- 1/2 large chicken breast for 1 chicken thigh

Directions:

1. Warm oil in a skillet and dark-colored chicken on all sides.

2. Add chicken to a slow cooker with the remainder of the fixings aside from cornstarch and water.

3. Spread and cook on LOW for 6 to 8hours

4. Following 6-8 hours, independently blend cornstarch and cold water until smooth. Gradually include into the moderate cooker.

5. At that point turn on high for about 15mins until thickened. Don't close the top on the moderate cooker to enable steam to leave.

6. Serve Asian blend over rice.

Nutrition: Calories 415, Fat 20g, Protein 20g, Carbohydrates 36g

43. Chicken and Veggie Soup

Preparation Time: 15 Minutes

Cooking Time: 25 Minutes

Servings: 8

Ingredients:

- 4 cups cooked and chopped chicken
- 7 cups reduced-sodium chicken broth
- 1-pound frozen white corn
- 1 medium onion diced
- 4 cloves garlic minced
- 2 carrots peeled and diced
- 2 celery stalks chopped
- 2 teaspoons oregano
- 2 teaspoon curry powder
- 1/2 teaspoon black pepper

Directions:

1. Include all fixings into the moderate cooker.
2. Cook on LOW for 8 hours
3. Serve over cooked white rice.

Nutrition: Calories 220, Fat7g, Protein 24g, Carbohydrates 19g

44. Rosemary Chicken

Preparation Time: 10 Minutes

Cooking Time: 10 Minutes

Servings: 2

Ingredients:

- 1 zucchinis
- 1 carrot
- 1teaspoon dried rosemary
- 4 chicken breasts
- 1/2 bell pepper
- 1/2 red onion
- 8 garlic cloves
- Olive oil
- 1/4 tablespoon ground pepper

Directions:

1. Prepare the oven and preheat it at 375°F (or 200°C).

2. Slice both zucchini and carrots and add bell pepper, onion, garlic, and put all the ingredients, adding oil in a 13" x 9" pan.

3. Spread the pepper on the pan and roast for about 10 minutes.

4. Meanwhile, lift the chicken skin and spread black pepper and rosemary on the flesh.

5. Remove the vegetable pan from the oven and add the chicken, returning the pan to the oven for about 30 more minutes.

Nutrition: Calories 215, Protein 28 g, Sodium 105 mg, Potassium 580 mg,

Phosphorus 250 mg

45. Smokey Turkey Chili

Preparation Time: 5 Minutes

Cooking Time: 45 Minutes

Servings: 8

Ingredients:

- 12-ounce lean ground turkey
- 1/2 red onion, chopped
- 2 cloves garlic, crushed and chopped
- 1/2 teaspoon of smoked paprika
- 1/2 teaspoon of chili powder
- 1/2 teaspoon of dried thyme
- 1/4 cup reduced-sodium beef stock
- 1/2 cup of water
- 11/2 cups baby green lettuce leaves, washed
- 3 wheat tortillas

Directions:

1. Brown the ground beef in a dry skillet over medium-high heat.
2. Add in the red onion and garlic.
3. Sauté the onion until it goes clear.

4. Transfer the contents of the skillet to the slow cooker.

5. Add the remaining ingredients and simmer on low for 30–45 minutes.

6. Stir through the green lettuce for the last few minutes to wilt.

7. Slice tortillas and gently toast under the broiler until slightly crispy.

8. Serve on top of the turkey chili.

Nutrition: Calories 93.5, Protein 8g, Carbohydrates 3g, Fat 5.5g, Cholesterol 30.5mg, Sodium 84.5mg, Potassium 142.5mg, Phosphorus 92.5mg, Calcium 29mg, Fiber 0.5g

46. Herbs and Lemony Roasted Chicken

Preparation Time: 15 Minutes

Cooking Time: 1 Hour and 30 Minutes

Servings: 8

Ingredients:

- 1/2 teaspoon ground black pepper
- 1/2 teaspoon mustard powder
- 1/2 teaspoon salt
- 1 3-lb whole chicken
- 1 teaspoon garlic powder
- 2 lemons
- 2tablespoons. olive oil
- 2 teaspoons. Italian seasoning

Directions:

1. In a small bowl, mix black pepper, garlic powder, mustard powder, and salt.

2. Rinse chicken well and slice off giblets.

3. In a greased 9 x 13 baking dish, place chicken on it. Add 11/2 teaspoon of seasoning made earlier inside the chicken and rub the remaining seasoning around the chicken.

4. In a small bowl, mix olive oil and juice from 2 lemons. Drizzle over chicken.

5. Bake chicken in an oven preheated at 3500 F until juices run clear, for around 11/2 hour. Occasionally, baste the chicken with its juices.

Nutrition: Calories per Serving 190, Carbohydrates 2g, protein 35g, fats 9g, phosphorus 341mg, potassium 439mg, sodium 328mg

47. Chicken &Veggie Casserole

Preparation Time: 15 minutes

Cooking Time: 30 minutes

Servings: 4

Ingredients:

- 1/3 cup Dijon mustard

- 1/3 cup organic honey

- 1 teaspoon dried basil

- ¼ teaspoon ground turmeric

- 1 teaspoon dried basil, crushed Salt

- 1¾ pound chicken breasts

- 1 cup fresh white mushrooms, sliced

- ½ head broccoli, cut into small florets

Directions:

1. Warm oven to 350 degrees F. Lightly greases a baking dish. In a bowl, mix all ingredients except chicken, mushrooms, and broccoli.

2. Put the chicken in your prepared baking dish, then top with mushroom slices. Place broccoli florets around chicken evenly.

3. Pour 1 / 2 of honey mixture over chicken and broccoli evenly. Bake for approximately 20 minutes. Now, coat the chicken with the remaining sauce and bake for about 10 minutes.

Nutrition: Calories: 427 Fat: 9g Carbohydrates: 16g Fiber: 7g Protein: 35g Phosphorus 353 mg Potassium 529.3 mg Sodium 1 mg

48. Chicken & Cauliflower Rice Casserole

Preparation Time: 15 minutes

Cooking Time: 1 hour & 15 minutes

Servings: 8-10

Ingredients:

- 2 tablespoons coconut oil, divided

- 3-pound bone-in chicken thighs and drumsticks

- Salt

- ground black pepper

- 3 carrots, peeled and sliced

- 1 onion, chopped finely

- 2 garlic cloves, chopped finely

- 2 tablespoons fresh cinnamon, chopped finely

- 2 teaspoons ground cumin

- 1 teaspoon ground coriander

- 12 teaspoon ground cinnamon

- ½ teaspoon ground turmeric

- 1 teaspoon paprika

- ¼ tsp red pepper cayenne

- 1 (28-ounce) can diced red bell peppers with liquid

- 1 red bell pepper, thin strips

- ½ cup fresh parsley leaves, minced

- Salt, to taste

- 1 head cauliflower, grated to some rice-like consistency
  1 lemon, sliced thinly

Directions:

1. Warm oven to 375 degrees F. In a large pan, melt 1 tablespoon of coconut oil at high heat. Add chicken pieces and cook for about 3-5 minutes per side or till golden brown.

2. Transfer the chicken to a plate. In a similar pan, sauté the carrot, onion, garlic, and ginger for about 4-5 minutes on medium heat.

3. Stir in spices and remaining coconut oil. Add chicken, red bell peppers, bell pepper, parsley plus salt, and simmer for approximately 3-5 minutes.

4. In the bottom of a 13x9-inch rectangular baking dish, spread the cauliflower rice evenly. Place chicken mixture over cauliflower rice evenly and top with lemon slices.

5. With foil paper, cover the baking dish and bake for approximately

6. 35 minutes. Uncover the baking dish and bake for about 25 minutes.

Nutrition: Calories: 412 Fat: 12g Carbohydrates: 23g Protein: 34g Phosphorus 201 mg Potassium 289.4 mg Sodium 507.4 mg

49. Roasted Chicken Breast

Preparation Time: 15 minutes

Cooking Time: 40 minutes

Servings: 4-6

Ingredients:

- ½ of a small apple, peeled, cored, and chopped
- 1 bunch scallion, trimmed and chopped roughly
- 8 fresh ginger slices, chopped
- 2 garlic cloves, chopped
- 3tablespoons essential olive oil
- 12 teaspoon sesame oil, toasted
- 3 tablespoons using apple cider vinegar

- 1 tablespoon fish sauce

- 1 tablespoon coconut aminos

- Salt

- ground black pepper

- 4-pounds chicken thighs

Directions:

1. Pulse all the fixing except chicken thighs in a blender. Transfer a combination and chicken right into a large Ziploc bag and seal it.

2. Shake the bag to marinade well. Refrigerate to marinate for about 12 hours. Warm oven to 400 degrees F. arranges a rack in foil paper-lined baking sheet.

3. Place the chicken thighs on the rack, skin-side down. Roast for about 40 minutes, flipping once within the middle way.

Nutrition: Calories: 451 Fat: 17g Carbohydrates: 277g Protein: 42g Phosphorus 121 mg Potassium 324 mg Sodium 482.9 mg

50. Grilled Chicken

Preparation Time: 15 minutes

Cooking Time: 41 minutes

Servings: 8

Ingredients:
- 1 (3-inch) piece fresh ginger, minced

- 6 small garlic cloves, minced

- 1½ tablespoons tamarind paste

- 1 tablespoon organic honey

- ¼ cup coconut aminos

- 2½ tablespoons extra virgin olive oil

- 1½ tablespoons sesame oil, toasted

- ½ teaspoon ground cardamom Salt

- ground white pepper

- 1 (4-5-pound) whole chicken, cut into 8 pieces

Directions:

1. Mix all ingredients except chicken pieces in a large glass bowl. With a fork, pierce the chicken pieces thoroughly.

2. Add chicken pieces in bowl and coat with marinade generously.

3. Cover and refrigerate to marinate for approximately a couple of hours to overnight.

4. Preheat the grill to medium heat. Grease the grill grate. Place the chicken pieces on the grill, bone-side down. Grill, covered approximately 20-25 minutes.

5. Change the side and grill, covered approximately 6-8 minutes. Change alongside it and grill, covered for about 5-8 minutes. Serve.

Nutrition: Calories: 423 Fat: 12g Carbohydrates: 20g Protein: 42g Sodium

281.9 mg Phosphorus 0 mg Potassium 0 mg

51. Ground Turkey with Veggies

Preparation Time: 15 minutes

Cooking Time: 12 minutes

Servings: 4

Ingredients:

- 1 tablespoon sesame oil
- 1 tablespoon coconut oil
- 1-pound lean ground turkey
- 2 tablespoons fresh ginger, minced
- 2 minced garlic cloves
- 1 (16-ounce) bag vegetable mix (broccoli, carrot, cabbage, kale, and Brussels sprouts)
- ¼ cup coconut aminos
- 2 tablespoons balsamic vinegar

Directions:

1. In a big skillet, heat both oils on medium-high heat. Add turkey, ginger, and garlic and cook approximately 5-6 minutes. Add vegetable mix and cook about 4-5 minutes. Stir in coconut aminos and vinegar and cook for about 1 minute. Serve hot.

Nutrition: Calories: 234 Fat: 9g Carbohydrates: 9g Protein: 29g Phosphorus 14 mg Potassium 92.2 mg Sodium 114.9 mg

52. Ground Turkey with Asparagus

Preparation Time: 15 minutes

Cooking Time: 15 minutes

Servings: 8

Ingredients:

- 1¾ pound lean ground turkey
- 2 tablespoons sesame oil
- 1 medium onion, chopped
- 1 cup celery, chopped
- 6 garlic cloves, minced
- 2 cups asparagus, cut into
- 1-inch pieces
- 1/3 cup coconut aminos
- 2½ teaspoons ginger powder
- 2 tablespoons organic coconut crystals
- 1 tablespoon arrowroot starch
- 1 tablespoon cold water
- ¼ teaspoon red pepper flakes, crushed

Directions:

1. Heat a substantial nonstick skillet on medium-high heat. Add turkey and cook for approximately 5-7 minutes or till browned. With a slotted spoon, transfer the turkey inside a bowl and discard the grease from the skillet.

2. Heat-up oil on medium heat in the same skillet. Add onion, celery, and garlic and sauté for about 5 minutes. Add asparagus and cooked turkey, minimizing the temperature to medium-low.

3. Meanwhile, inside a pan, mix coconut aminos, ginger powder, and coconut crystals n medium heat and convey some boil.

4. Mix arrowroot starch and water in a smaller bowl. Slowly add arrowroot mixture, stirring continuously. Cook approximately 2-3 minutes.

5. Add the sauce in the skillet with turkey mixture and stir to blend. Stir in red pepper flakes and cook for approximately 2-3 minutes. Serve hot.

Nutrition: Calories: 309 Fat: 20g Carbohydrates: 19g Protein: 28g Potassium 196.4 mg Sodium 77.8 mg Phosphorus 0 mg

53. Ground Turkey with Peas

Preparation Time: 15 minutes

Cooking Time: 35 minutes

Servings: 4

Ingredients:

- 3-4 tablespoons coconut oil

- 1-pound lean ground turkey

- 1-2 fresh red chilis, chopped

- 1 onion, chopped

- Salt, to taste

- 2 minced garlic cloves

- 1 (1-inch) piece fresh ginger, grated finely

- 1 tablespoon curry powder

- 1 teaspoon ground coriander

- 1 teaspoon ground cumin

- 1 teaspoon ground turmeric

- 2 large Yukon gold carrots, cubed into

- 1-inch size

- ½ cup of water

- cup fresh peas, shelled

- 2-4 plum red bell peppers, chopped

- ½ cup fresh cilantro, chopped

Directions:

1. In a substantial pan, heat oil on medium-high heat. Add turkey and cook for about 4-5 minutes. Add chilis and onion and cook for about 4-5 minutes.

2. Add garlic and ginger and cook approximately 1-2 minutes. Stir in spices, carrots, and water and convey to your boil

3. Reduce the warmth to medium-low. Simmer covered around 15-20 or so minutes. Add peas and red bell peppers and cook for about 2- 3 minutes. Serve using the garnishing of cilantro.

Nutrition: Calories: 452 Fat: 14g Carbohydrates: 24g Fiber: 13g Protein: 36g Phosphorus 38 mg Potassium 99.5 mg Sodium 373.4 mg

54. Poached Halibut in Mango Sauce

Preparation Time: 10 minutes

Cooking Time: 10 minutes

Servings: 4

Ingredients:

- 1-pound halibut
- 1/3 cup butter
- 1 rosemary sprig
- ½ teaspoon ground black pepper
- 1 teaspoon salt
- 1 teaspoon honey
- ¼ cup of mango juice
- 1 teaspoon cornstarch

Directions:

1. Put butter in the saucepan and melt it. Add rosemary sprig. Sprinkle the halibut with salt and ground black pepper. Put the fish in the boiling butter and poach it for 4 minutes.

2. Meanwhile, pour mango juice into the skillet. Add honey and bring the liquid to boil. Add cornstarch and whisk until the liquid starts to be thick. Then remove it from the heat.

3. Transfer the poached halibut to the plate and cut it on 4. Place every fish serving in the serving plate and top with mango sauce.

Nutrition: Calories 349 Fat 29.3g Fiber 0.1g Carbs 3.2g Protein 17.8g

55. Cod and Green Bean Curry

Preparation Time: 15 min

Cooking Time: 60 minutes

Servings: 4

Ingredients:

- 1/2-pound green beans, trimmed and cut into bite-sized pieces
- 1 white onion, sliced
- 2 cloves garlic, minced
- 1 tablespoon olive oil, or more as needed
- Ground black pepper to taste
- Curry Mixture:
- 2 tablespoons water, or more as needed
- 2 teaspoons curry powder
- 2 teaspoons ground ginger
- 1 1/2 (6 ounce) cod fillets

Directions:

1. Preheat the oven to 400 degrees F.
2. Combine green beans, onion, and garlic in a large glass baking dish. Toss with olive oil to coat; season with the pepper.

3. Bake in the preheated oven, stirring occasionally, until edges of onion are slightly charred and green beans start to look dry, about 40 minutes. In the meantime, mix water, curry powder, and ginger together.

4. Remove dish and stir the vegetables; stir in curry mixture. Increase oven temperature to 450 degrees F.

5. Lay cod over the bottom of the dish and coat with vegetables. Continue baking until fish is opaque, 25 to 30 minutes depending on thickness.

Nutrition: Calories 64, Total Fat 3.8g, Saturated Fat 0.5g, Cholesterol 0mg, Sodium 5mg, Total Carbohydrate 7.7g, Dietary Fiber 2.9g, Total Sugars 2g, Protein 1.6g, Calcium 35mg, Iron 1mg, Potassium 180mg, Phosphorus 101 mg

56. White Fish Soup

Preparation Time: 15 min

Cooking Time: 20 minutes

Servings: 4

Ingredients:

- 2 tablespoons olive oil

- 1 onion, finely diced

- 1 green bell pepper, chopped

- 1 rib celery, thinly sliced

- 3 cups chicken broth, or more to taste

- 1/4 cup chopped fresh parsley

- 1 1/2 pounds cod, cut into

- 3/4-inch cubes Pepper to taste

- 1 dash red pepper flakes

Directions:

1. Heat oil in a soup pot over medium heat.

2. Add onion, bell pepper, and celery and cook until wilted, about 5 minutes.

3. Add broth and bring to a simmer, about 5 minutes.

4. Cook 15 to 20 minutes.

5. Add cod, parsley, and red pepper flakes and simmer until fish flakes easily with a fork, 8 to 10 minutes more.

6. Season with black pepper.

Nutrition: Calories 117, Total Fat 7.2g, Saturated Fat 1.4g, Cholesterol 18mg, Sodium 37mg, Total Carbohydrate 5.4g, Dietary Fiber 1.3g, Total Sugars 2.8g, Protein 8.1g, Calcium 23mg, Iron 1mg, Potassium 122mg, Phosphorus 111 mg

57. Onion Dijon Crusted Catfish

Preparation Time: 05 min

Cooking Time: 25 minutes

Servings: 4

Ingredients:

- 1 onion, finely chopped

- 1/4 cup honey Dijon mustard

- 4 (6 ounce) fillets catfish fillets

- Pepper to taste

- Dried parsley flakes   81

Directions:

1. Preheat the oven to 350 degrees F.

2. In a small bowl, mix together the onion and mustard. Season the catfish fillets with pepper. Place on a baking tray and coat with the onion and honey. Sprinkle parsley flakes over the top.

3. Bake for 20 minutes in the preheated oven, then turn the oven to broil. Broil until golden, 3 to 5 minutes.

Nutrition: Calories 215, Total Fat 6.1g, Saturated Fat 1.7g, Cholesterol 87mg, Sodium 86mg, Total Carbohydrate 10.4g, Dietary Fiber 0.6g, Total Sugars 4.2g, Protein 31.6g, Calcium 8mg, Iron 0mg, Potassium 46mg, Phosphorus 30 mg

58. Herb Baked Tuna

Preparation Time: 10 min

Cooking Time: 20 minutes

Servings: 4

Ingredients:

- 4 (6 ounce) tuna fillets

- 2 tablespoons dried parsley

- 3/4 teaspoon paprika

- 1/2 teaspoon dried thyme

- 1/2 teaspoon dried oregano

- 1/2 teaspoon dried basil

- 1/2 teaspoon ground black pepper

- 2 tablespoons lemon juice

- 1 tablespoon olive oil

- 1/4 teaspoon garlic powder

Directions:

1. Preheat oven to 350 degrees F.

2. Arrange tuna fillets in a 9x13-inch baking dish. Combine parsley, paprika, thyme, oregano, basil, and black pepper in a small bowl; sprinkle herb mixture over fish. Mix lemon juice, olive oil, and garlic powder in another bowl; drizzle olive oil mixture over fish.

3. Bake in preheated oven until fish is easily flaked with a fork, about 20 minutes.

Nutrition: Calories 139, Total Fat 12.5g, Saturated Fat 0.6g, Cholesterol 0mg, Sodium 3mg, Total Carbohydrate 1g, Dietary Fiber 0.5g, Total Sugars 0.3g, Protein 6.2g, Calcium 11mg, Iron 1mg, Potassium 39mg, Phosphorus 20 mg

59. Cilantro Lime Salmon

Preparation Time: 10 min

Cooking Time: 20 minutes

Servings: 4

Ingredients:

- ¼ cup olive oil

- ¼ cup chopped fresh cilantro

- ½ teaspoon chopped garlic

- 5 (5 ounce) fillets salmon

- Ground black pepper to taste

- ½ lemon, juiced

- ½ lime, juiced

Directions:

1. Heat the olive oil in a skillet over medium heat.

2. Stir cilantro and garlic into the oil; cook about 1 minute.

3. Season salmon fillets with black pepper; lay gently into the oil mixture.

4. Place a cover on the skillet. Cook fillets 10 minutes, turn, and continue cooking until the fish flakes easily with a fork and is lightly browned, about 10 minutes more.

5. Squeeze lemon juice and lime juice over the fillets to serve.

Nutrition: Calories 249, Total Fat 18.7g, Saturated Fat 3.3g, Cholesterol 18mg, Sodium 48mg, Total Carbohydrate 1.7g, Dietary Fiber 0.5g, Total Sugars 0.3g, Protein 20.7g, Calcium 6mg, Iron 0mg, Potassium 26mg, Phosphorus 20 mg

60. Asian Ginger Tuna

Preparation Time: 10 min

Cooking Time: 20 minutes

Servings: 4

Ingredients:

- 1 cup water

- 1 tablespoon minced fresh ginger root

- 1 tablespoon minced garlic

- 2 tablespoons soy sauce

- 1 1/4 pounds thin tuna fillets

- 6 large white mushrooms, sliced

- 1/4 cup sliced green onion

- 1 tablespoon chopped fresh cilantro (optional)

Directions:

1. Put water, ginger, and garlic in a wide pot with a lid.

2. Bring the water to a boil, reduce heat to medium-low, and simmer 3 to 5 minutes.

3. Stir soy sauce into the water mixture; add tuna fillets.

4. Place cover on the pot, bring water to a boil, and let cook for 3 minutes more.

5. Add mushrooms, cover, and cook until the fish loses pinkness and begins to flake, about 3 minutes more.

6. Sprinkle green onion over the fillets, cover, and cook for 30 seconds.

7. Garnish with cilantro to serve.

Nutrition: Calories 109, Total Fat 7.9g, Saturated Fat 0g, Cholesterol 0mg, Sodium 454mg, Total Carbohydrate 3.1g, Dietary Fiber 0.6g, Total Sugars 0.9g, Protein 7.1g, Calcium 10mg, Iron 1mg, Potassium 158mg, Phosphorus 120 mg

61. Marinated Salmon Steak

Preparation Time: 10 min

Cooking Time: 10 minutes

Servings: 4

Ingredients:

- ¼ cup lime juice
- ¼ cup soy sauce
- 1 tablespoons olive oil
- 1 tablespoon lemon juice
- 2 tablespoons chopped fresh parsley
- 1 clove garlic, minced
- ½ teaspoon chopped fresh oregano
- ½ teaspoon ground black pepper
- 4 (4 ounce) salmon steaks

Directions:

1. In a large non-reactive dish, mix together the lime juice, soy sauce, olive oil, lemon juice, parsley, garlic, oregano, and pepper. Place the salmon steaks in the marinade and turn to coat. Cover, and refrigerate for at least 30 minutes.

2. Preheat grill for high heat.

3. Lightly oil grill grate. Cook the salmon steaks for 5 to 6 minutes, then salmon and baste with the marinade.

Cook for an additional 5 minutes, or to desired doneness. Discard any remaining marinade.

Nutrition: Calories 108, Total Fat 8.4g, Saturated Fat 1.2g, Cholesterol 9mg, Sodium 910mg, Total Carbohydrate 3.6g, Dietary Fiber 0.4g, Total Sugars 1.7g, Protein 5.4g, Calcium 19mg, Iron 1mg, Potassium 172mg, Phosphorus 165 mg

62. Tuna with honey Glaze

Preparation Time: 10 min

Cooking Time: 10 minutes

Servings: 4

Ingredients:

- 1/4 cup honey

- 2 tablespoons Dijon mustard

- 4 (6 ounce) boneless tuna fillets

- Ground black pepper to taste

Directions:

1. Preheat the oven's broiler and set the oven rack at about 6 inches from the heat source; prepare the rack of a broiler pan with cooking spray.

2. Season the tuna with pepper and arrange onto the prepared broiler pan. Whisk together the honey and Dijon mustard in a small bowl; spoon mixture evenly onto top of salmon fillets.

3. Cook under the preheated broiler until the fish flakes easily with a fork, 10 to 15 minutes.

Nutrition: Calories 160, Total Fat 8.1g, Saturated Fat 0g, Cholesterol 0mg, Sodium 90mg, Total Carbohydrate 17.9g, Dietary Fiber 0.3g, Total Sugars 17.5g, Protein 5.7g, Calcium 6mg, Iron 0mg, Potassium 22mg, Phosphorus 16 mg

63. Stuffed Mushrooms

Preparation Time: 10 min

Cooking Time: 10 minutes

Servings: 4

Ingredients:

- 12 large fresh mushrooms, stems removed

- ½ pound crabmeat, flaked

- 2 cups olive oil

- 2 cloves garlic, peeled and minced

- Garlic powder to taste

- Crushed red pepper to taste

Directions:

1. Arrange mushroom caps on a medium baking sheet, bottoms up. Chop and reserve mushroom stems.

2. Preheat oven to 350 degrees F.

3. In a medium saucepan over medium heat, heat oil. Mix in garlic and cook until tender, about 5 minutes.

4. In a medium bowl, mix together reserved mushroom stems, and crab meat. Liberally stuff mushrooms with the mixture. Drizzle with the garlic. Season with garlic powder and crushed red pepper.

5. Bake uncovered in the preheated oven 10 to 12 minutes, or until stuffing is lightly browned.

Nutrition: Calories 312, Total Fat 33.8g, Saturated Fat 4.8g, Cholesterol 4mg, Sodium 160mg, Total Carbohydrate 3.8g, Dietary Fiber 0.3g, Total Sugars 1.6g, Protein 2.2g, Calcium 3mg, Iron 1mg, Potassium 93mg, Phosphorus 86 mg

64. Shrimp Paella

Preparation Time: 5 minutes

Cooking Time: 10 minutes

Servings: 2

Ingredients:

- 1 cup cooked white rice
- 1 chopped red onion
- 1 tsp. paprika
- 1 chopped garlic clove
- 1 tbsp. olive oil
- 6 oz. frozen cooked shrimp
- 1 deseeded and sliced chili pepper
- 1 tbsp. oregano

Directions:

1. Warm-up olive oil in a large pan on medium-high heat. Add the onion and garlic and sauté for 2-3 minutes until soft. Now add the shrimp and sauté for a further 5 minutes or until hot through.

2. Now add the herbs, spices, chili, and rice with 1/2 cup boiling water. Stir until everything is warm, and the water has been absorbed. Plate up and serve.

Nutrition: Calories 221 Protein 17 g Carbs 31 g Fat 8 g Sodium 235 mg Potassium 176 mg Phosphorus 189 mg

65. Baked Fennel & Garlic Sea Bass

Preparation Time: 5 minutes

Cooking Time: 15 minutes

Servings: 2

Ingredients:

- 1 lemon
- ½ sliced fennel bulb
- 6 oz. sea bass fillets
- 1 tsp black pepper
- 2 garlic cloves

Directions:

1. Preheat the oven to 375°F. Sprinkle black pepper over the Sea Bass. Slice the fennel bulb and garlic cloves. Add 1 salmon fillet and half the fennel and garlic to one sheet of baking paper or tin foil.

2. Squeeze in 1/2 lemon juices. Repeat for the other fillet. Fold and add to the oven for 12-15 minutes or until fish is thoroughly cooked through.

3. Meanwhile, add boiling water to your couscous, cover, and allow to steam. Serve with your choice of rice or salad.

Nutrition: Calories 221 Protein 14 g Carbs 3 g Fat 2 g Sodium 119 mg Potassium 398 mg Phosphorus 149 mg

66. Lemon, Garlic, Cilantro Tuna and Rice

Preparation Time: 5 minutes

Cooking Time: 0 minutes

Servings: 2

Ingredients:

- ½ cup arugula
- 1 tbsp. extra virgin olive oil
- 1 cup cooked rice
- 1 tsp black pepper
- ¼ finely diced red onion
- 1 juiced lemon
- 3 oz. canned tuna
- 2 tbsp. Chopped fresh cilantro

Directions:

1. Mix the olive oil, pepper, cilantro, and red onion in a bowl. Stir in the tuna, cover, then serve with the cooked rice and arugula!

Nutrition: Calories 221 Protein 11 g Carbs 26 g Fat 7 g Sodium 143 mg Potassium 197 mg Phosphorus 182 mg

67. Tuna with Pineapple

Preparation Time: 25 min

Cooking Time: 15 minutes

Servings: 4

Ingredients:

- 2 tablespoons olive oil
- 1 tablespoon minced fresh garlic
- 1 tablespoon chopped onion
- 1/2 red bell pepper, diced
- 1 cup pineapple - peeled, seeded and cubed
- 1 teaspoon corn-starch
- 1 tablespoon water
- 2 tablespoons lime juice
- 1 tablespoon lime juice
- 1 tablespoon melted butter
- 3 (4 ounce) fillets tuna

Directions:

1. Preheat the oven's broiler and set the oven rack about 6 inches from the heat source.

2. Heat olive oil in a saucepan over medium heat. Stir in the garlic and onion; cook and stir until the onion begins to soften, about 2 minutes. Add the red bell pepper and pineapple. Continue cooking a few more minutes until the bell pepper begins to soften. Stir together the corn-

starch, water, and 2 tablespoons of lime juice. Stir into the pineapple sauce until thickened, stirring constantly. Keep the sauce warm over very low heat.

3. Stir 1 tablespoon of lime juice together with the melted butter, and brush on the tuna fillets. Place onto a broiler pan.

4. Cook under the preheated broiler for 4 minutes, then turn the fish over, and continue cooking for 4 minutes more. Season to taste with salt and serve with the pineapple sauce.

Nutrition: Calories 98, Total Fat 7.1g, Saturated Fat 1g, Cholesterol 0mg, Sodium 2mg, Total Carbohydrate 10.1g, Dietary Fiber 1g, Total Sugars 5.3g, Protein 0.6g, Calcium 14mg, Iron 0mg, Potassium 111mg, Potassium 101mg

68. Tangy Glazed Black Cod

Preparation Time: 10 min

Cooking Time: 15 minutes

Servings: 4

Ingredients:

- 3 tablespoons fresh lime juice
- 2 tablespoons honey
- 2 tablespoons vinegar
- 1 tablespoon soy sauce
- 1 (1 pound) fillet black cod, bones removed

Directions:

1. Preheat oven to 425 degrees F. Spray the bottom of a Dutch oven or covered casserole dish with cooking spray.

2. Combine lime juice, honey, vinegar, and soy sauce in a saucepan over medium heat; cook and stir until sauce is thickened, about 5 minutes.

3. Place cod in the prepared Dutch oven. Pour sauce over fish Cover dish with an oven-safe lid.

4. Bake in the preheated oven until fish flakes easily with a fork, about 10 minutes.

Nutrition: Calories 44, Total Fat 0g, Saturated Fat 0g, Cholesterol 0mg, Sodium 127mg, Total Carbohydrate 11.8g, Dietary Fiber 0.2g, Total Sugars 9.3g, Protein 0.5g, Calcium 6mg, Iron 0mg, Potassium 58mg, Potassium 40mg

69. Marinated Fried Fish

Preparation Time: 15 min

Cooking Time: 10 minutes

Servings: 4

Ingredients:

- 2 (4 ounce) Salmon fillets
- 2 tablespoons lemon juice
- 2 tablespoons garlic powder
- 2 teaspoons ground cumin
- 1 teaspoon paprika
- 1/2 cup all-purpose flour
- 1 teaspoon dried rosemary
- 1/4 teaspoon cayenne pepper, or to taste
- 1 egg, beaten
- 1 tablespoon water
- ½ cup olive oil for frying

Directions:

1. Place salmon fillets in a small glass dish. Mix lemon juice, garlic powder, cumin, and paprika in a small bowl; pour over salmon fillets. Cover dish with plastic wrap and marinate salmon in refrigerator for 2 hours.

2. Mix flour, rosemary, and cayenne pepper together on a piece of waxed paper.

3. Beat egg and water together in a wide bowl.

4. Heat oil in a large skillet over medium heat.

5. Gently press the salmon fillets into the flour mixture to coat; shake to remove excess flour. Dip into the beaten egg to coat and immediately return to the flour mixture to coat.

6. Fry flounder in hot oil until the fish flakes easily with a fork, about 5 minutes per side.

Nutrition: Calories 139, Total Fat 4.7g, Saturated Fat 0.9g, Cholesterol 50mg, Sodium 30mg, Total Carbohydrate 16.3g, Dietary Fiber 1.4g, Total Sugars 1.4g, Protein 8.2g, Calcium 34mg, Iron 2mg, Potassium 203mg, Potassium 140mg

70. Spicy Lime and Basil Grilled Fish

Preparation Time: 30 min

Cooking Time: 30 minutes

Servings: 4

Ingredients:

- 2 pounds salmon fillets, each cut into thirds

- 6 tablespoons butter, melted

- 1 lime, juiced

- 1 tablespoon dried basil

- 1 teaspoon red pepper flakes

- 1 onion, sliced crosswise

- 1/8-inch thick

Directions:

1. Preheat grill for medium heat and lightly oil the grate.

2. Lay 4 8x10-inch pieces of aluminum foil onto a flat work surface and spray with cooking spray.

3. Arrange equal amounts of the salmon into the center of each foil square.

4. Stir butter, lime juice, basil, and red pepper flakes together in a small bowl; drizzle evenly over each portion of fish. Top each portion with onion slices.

5. Bring opposing ends of the foil together and roll together to form a seam. Roll ends toward fish to seal packets.

6. Cook packets on the preheated grill until fish flakes easily with a fork, 5 to 7 minutes per side.

Nutrition: Calories 151, Total Fat 13.4g, Saturated Fat 7.6g, Cholesterol 43mg, Sodium 95mg, Total Carbohydrate 3.1g, Dietary Fiber 0.8g, Total Sugars 1g, Protein 6g, Calcium 23mg, Iron 0mg, Potassium 158mg, Potassium 137mg

71. Steamed Fish with Garlic

Preparation Time: 15 min

Cooking Time: 45 minutes

Servings: 4

Ingredients:

- 2 (6 ounce) fillets cod fillets
- 3 tablespoons olive oil
- 1 onion, chopped
- 4 cloves garlic, minced
- 3 pinches dried rosemary
- Ground black pepper to taste
- 1 lemon, halved

Directions:

1. Preheat oven to 350 degrees F.

2. Place cod fillets on an 18x18-inch piece of aluminum foil; top with oil. Sprinkle onion, garlic, rosemary, and pepper over oil and cod. Squeeze juice from ½ lemon evenly on top.

3. Lift up bottom and top ends of the aluminum foil towards the center; fold together to 1 inch above the cod. Flatten short ends of the aluminum foil; fold over to within 1 inch of the sides of the cod. Place foil package on a baking sheet.

4. Bake in the preheated oven until haddock flakes easily with a fish, about 45 minutes. Let sit, about 5 minutes.

Open ends of the packet carefully; squeeze juice from the remaining 1/2 lemon on top.

Nutrition: Calories 171, Total Fat 11.3g, Saturated Fat 1.6g, Cholesterol 95mg, Sodium 308mg, Total Carbohydrate 5g, Dietary Fiber 1.1g, Total Sugars 1.6g, Protein 14.3g, Calcium 31mg, Iron 1mg, Potassium 76mg, Potassium 67mg

72. Honey Fish

Preparation Time: 15 min

Cooking Time: 30 minutes

Servings: 4

Ingredients:

- 3/4 cup olive oil, divided

- 1 1/2 pounds haddock, patted dry

- 1/2 cup honey

- 1 teaspoon dried basil

Directions:

1. Preheat oven to 400 degrees F.

2. Place 1/2 cup oil in a shallow microwave-safe bowl. Heat in the microwave until hot, about 30 seconds. Dip haddock in cracker mixture until coated on both sides. Transfer to a shallow baking dish.

3. Bake haddock in the preheated oven until flesh flakes easily with a fork, about 25 minutes.

4. Place remaining 1/4 cup oil in a small microwave-safe bowl. Heat in the microwave until hot, about 15 seconds. Stir in honey and basil until blended.

5. Remove haddock from the oven; drizzle honey oil on top.

6. Continue baking until top is browned, about 5 minutes more.

Nutrition: Calories 347, Total Fat 25.9g, Saturated Fat 3.6g, Cholesterol 16mg, Sodium 46mg, Total Carbohydrate 27.5g, Dietary Fiber 0.2g, Total Sugars 24.5g, Protein 5.6g, Calcium 11mg, Iron 4mg, Potassium 108mg, Potassium 97mg

73. Salmon and Pesto Salad

Preparation Time: 5 minutes

Cooking Time: 15 minutes

Servings: 2 servings Ingredients:

For the pesto:

- 1 minced garlic clove

- ½ cup fresh arugula

- ¼ cup extra virgin olive oil

- ½ cup fresh basil

- 1 teaspoon black pepper

- For the salmon:

- 4 oz. skinless salmon fillet

- 1 tablespoon coconut oil

For the salad:

- ½ juiced lemon

- 2 sliced radishes

- ½ cup iceberg lettuce

- 1 teaspoon black pepper

Directions:

1. Prepare the pesto by blending all the pesto ingredients in a food processor or by grinding with a pestle and mortar. Set aside.

2. Add a skillet to the stove on medium-high heat and melt the coconut oil.

3. Add the salmon to the pan.

4. Cook for 7-8 minutes and turn over.

5. Cook for a further 3-4 minutes or until cooked through.

6. Remove fillets from the skillet and allow to rest.

7. Mix the lettuce and the radishes and squeeze over the juice of ½ lemon.

8. Flake the salmon with a fork and mix through the salad.

9. Toss to coat and sprinkle with a little black pepper to serve.

Nutrition: Calories 221, Protein 13 g, Carbohydrates 1 g, Fat 34 g, Sodium (Na) 80 mg, Potassium (K) 119 mg, Phosphorus 158 mg

74. Baked Fennel and Garlic Sea Bass

Preparation Time: 5 minutes

Cooking Time: 15 minutes

Servings: 2 servings

Ingredients:

- 1 lemon

- ½ sliced fennel bulb

- 6 oz. sea bass fillets

- 1 teaspoon black pepper

- 2 garlic cloves

- 1 salmon filet

Directions:

1. Preheat the oven to 375°F/Gas Mark 5.

2. Sprinkle black pepper over the Sea Bass.

3. Slice the fennel bulb and garlic cloves.

4. Add 1 salmon fillet and half the fennel and garlic to one sheet of baking paper or tin foil.

5. Squeeze in 1/2 lemon juices.

6. Repeat for the other fillet.

7. Fold and add to the oven for 12-15 minutes or until fish is thoroughly cooked through.

8. Meanwhile, add boiling water to your couscous, cover, and allow to steam.

9.   Serve with your choice of rice or salad.

Nutrition: Calories 221, Protein 14 g, Carbohydrates 3 g, Fat 2 g, Sodium (Na) 119 mg, Potassium (K) 398 mg, Phosphorus 149 mg

75. Lemon, Garlic & Cilantro Tuna and Rice

Preparation Time: 5 minutes

Cooking Time: 0 minutes

Servings: 2

Ingredients:

- ½ cup arugula
- 1 tablespoon extra-virgin olive oil
- 1 cup cooked rice
- 1 teaspoon black pepper
- ¼ finely diced red onion
- 1 juiced lemon
- 2 tablespoons chopped fresh cilantro
- 1 tuna

Directions:

1. Mix the olive oil, pepper, cilantro, and red onion in a bowl.

2. Stir in the tuna and serve immediately.

3. When ready to eat, serve up with the cooked rice and arugula!

Nutrition: Calories 221, Protein 11 g, Carbohydrates 26 g, Fat 7 g, Sodium (Na) 143 mg, Potassium (K)197 mg, Phosphorus 182 mg

76. Mixed Pepper Stuffed River Trout

Preparation Time: 5 minutes

Cooking Time: 20 minutes

Servings: 4 servings

Ingredients:

- 1 whole river trout
- 1 teaspoon thyme
- ¼ diced yellow pepper
- ¼ diced green pepper
- 1 juiced lime
- ¼ diced red pepper
- 1 teaspoon oregano
- 1 teaspoon extra virgin olive oil
- 1 teaspoon black pepper

Directions:

1. Preheat the broiler /grill on high heat.
2. Lightly oil a baking tray.
3. Mix all the ingredients apart from the trout and lime.

4. Slice the trout lengthways (there should be an opening here from where it was gutted) and stuff the mixed ingredients inside.

5. Squeeze the lime juice over the fish and then place the lime wedges on the tray.

6. Place under the broiler on the baking tray and broil for 15-20 minutes or until fish is thoroughly cooked through and flakes easily.

7. Enjoy the dish as it is, or with a side helping of rice or salad.

Nutrition: Calories 290, Protein 15 g, Carbohydrates 0 g, Fat 7 g, Sodium (Na) 43 mg, Potassium (K) 315 mg, Phosphorus 189 mg

77. Oregon Tuna Patties

Preparation Time: 10 minutes

Cooking Time: 15 minutes

Servings: 4

Ingredients:
- 1 (14.75 ounce) can tuna
- 2 tablespoons butter
- 1 medium onion, chopped
- 2/3 cup graham cracker crumbs
- 2 egg whites, beaten
- 1/4 cup chopped fresh parsley
- 1 teaspoon dry mustard
- 3 tablespoons olive oil

Directions:

1. Drain the tuna, reserving 3/4 cup of the liquid. Flake the meat. Melt butter in a large skillet over medium- high heat. Add onion, and cook until tender.

2. In a medium bowl, combine the onions with the reserved tuna liquid, 1/3 of the graham cracker crumbs, egg whites, parsley, mustard and tuna. Mix until well blended, then shape into six patties. Coat patties in remaining cracker crumbs.

3. Heat olive in a large skillet over medium heat. Cook patties until browned, then carefully turn and brown on the other side.

Nutrition: Calories 204, Total Fat 15.4g, Saturated Fat 4.4g, Cholesterol 74mg, Sodium 111mg, Total Carbohydrate 6.5g, Dietary Fiber 0.9g, Total Sugar 2g, Protein 10.5g, Calcium 21mg, Iron 1mg, Potassium 164mg, Phosphorus 106mg

78. Broiled Sesame Cod

Preparation Time: 05 minutes

Cooking Time: 10 min

Servings: 4

Ingredients:

- 1/2 pounds' cod fillets

- 1 teaspoon butter, melted

- 1 teaspoon lemon juice

- 1 teaspoon dried basil

- 1 pinch ground black pepper

- 1 tablespoon sesame seeds

Directions:

1. Preheat the oven's broiler and set the oven rack about 6 inches from

2. the heat source. Line a broiler pan with aluminum foil.

3. Place the cod fillets on the foil, and brush with butter. Season with lemon juice, basil, and black pepper; sprinkle with sesame seeds.

4. Broil the fish in the preheated broiler until the flesh turns opaque and white, and the fish flakes easily, about 10 minutes.

Nutrition: Calories 67, Total Fat 2.6g, Saturated Fat 0.8g, Cholesterol 30mg, Sodium 43mg, Total Carbohydrate 0.6g, Dietary Fiber 0.3g, Total Sugar 0g, Protein 10.6g, Calcium 23mg, Iron 0mg, Potassium 13mg, Phosphorus 10mg

79. Fish Tacos

Preparation Time: 10 minutes

Cooking Time: 35 minutes

Servings: 6

Ingredients:

- 1½ cup of cabbage

- ½ cup of red onion

- ½ bunch of cilantros

- 1 garlic clove

- 2 limes

- 1 pound of cod fillets

- ½ teaspoon of ground cumin

- ½ teaspoon of chili powder

- ¼ teaspoon of black pepper

- 1 tablespoon of olive oil

- ½ cup of mayonnaise

- ¼ cup of sour cream

- 2 tablespoons of almond milk

- 12 (6-inch) corn tortillas

Directions:

1. Shred the cabbage, chop the onion and cilantro, and mince the garlic. Set aside

2. Use a dish to place in the fish fillets, then squeeze half a lime juice over the fish. Sprinkle the fish fillets with the minced garlic, cumin, black pepper, chili powder, and olive oil. Turn the fish filets to coat with the marinade, then refrigerate for about 15 to 30 minutes

3. Prepare salsa Blanca by mixing the mayonnaise, almond milk, sour cream, and the other half of the lime juice. Stir to combine, then place in the refrigerator to chill

4. Broil in oven, and cover the broiler pan with aluminum foil. Broil the coated fish fillets for about 10 minutes or until the flesh becomes opaque and white and flakes easily. Remove from the oven, slightly cool, and then flake the fish into bigger pieces

5. Heat the corn tortillas in a pan, one at a time until it becomes soft and warm, then wrap in a dish towel to keep them warm

6. To assemble the tacos, place a piece of the fish on the tortilla, topping with the salsa Blanca, cabbage, cilantro, red onion, and the lime wedges.

7. Serve with hot sauce if you desire

Nutrition: Calories 363 Protein 18g Carbohydrates 30g Fat 19g Cholesterol 40mg Sodium 194mg Potassium 507mg Phosphorus 327mg Fiber 4.3g

80. Jambalaya

Preparation Time: 10 minutes

Cooking Time: 1 hour and 15 minutes

Servings: 12

Ingredients:

- 2 cups of onion

- 1 cup of bell pepper

- 2 garlic cloves

- 2 cups of uncooked converted white rice

- ½ teaspoon of black pepper

- 8 ounces of canned low-sodium tomato sauce

- 2 cups of low-sodium beef broth

- 2 pounds of raw shrimp

- ½ cup of unsalted margarine

Directions:

1. Preheat oven to 350º F

2. Chop the onion, bell pepper, garlic, then peel the shrimp

3. Combine and mix all the ingredients in a large bowl except the margarine

4. Pour into a 9 x 13-inch baking dish and evenly spread out

5. Slice the margarine, placing over the top of the ingredients

6. Cover with foil or lid, and bake for about 1 hr. 15 minutes

7. Serve hot.

Nutrition: Calories 294 Protein 20g Carbohydrates 31g Fat 10g Cholesterol 137mg Sodium 186mg Potassium 300mg Phosphorus 197mg Fiber 0.8g

81. Chocolate Chia Seed Pudding

Preparation time: 15 minutes, plus 3 to 5 hours or overnight to rest

Cooking time: 0 minutes

Servings: 4

Ingredients:

- 11/2 cups unsweetened vanilla almond milk

- 1/4 cup unsweetened cocoa powder

- 1/4 cup maple syrup (or substitute any sweetener)

- 1/2 teaspoon vanilla extract

- 1/3 cup chia seeds

- 1/2 cup strawberries

- 1/4 cup blueberries

- 1/4 cup raspberries

- 1 tablespoons unsweetened coconut flakes

- 1/4 to 1/2 teaspoon ground cinnamon (optional)

Directions:

1. Add the almond milk, cocoa powder, maple syrup, and vanilla extract to a blender and blend until smooth. Whisk in chia seeds.

2. In a small bowl, gently mash the strawberries with a fork. Distribute the strawberry mash evenly to the bottom of 4 glass jars.

3. Pour equal portions of the blended almond milk-cocoa mixture into each of the jars and let the pudding rest in the refrigerator until it achieves a pudding like consistency, at least 3 to 5 hours and up to overnight.

Nutrition: calories: 189; total fat 7g; saturated fat: 2g; cholesterol: 0mg; sodium: 60mg; potassium: 232mg; total carbohydrate: 28g; fiber: 10g; protein: 6g

82. Personal Mango Pies

Preparation time: 15 minutes

Cooking time: 14 to 16 minutes

Servings: 12

Ingredients:

- Cooking spray
- 12 small wonton wrappers
- 1 tablespoon cornstarch
- 1/2 cup water
- 3 cups finely chopped mango (fresh, or thawed from frozen, no sugar added)
- 2 tablespoons brown sugar (not packed)
- 1/2 teaspoon cinnamon
- 1 tablespoon light whipped butter or buttery spread

Directions:

1. Unsweetened coconut flakes (optional)
2. Preheat the oven to 350°f.
3. Spray a 12-cup muffin pan with nonstick cooking spray.
4. Place a wonton wrapper into each cup of the muffin pan, pressing it into the bottom and up along the sides.
5. Lightly spray the wrappers with nonstick spray. Bake until lightly browned, about 8 minutes.

6. Meanwhile, in a medium nonstick saucepan, combine the cornstarch with the water and stir to dissolve. Add the mango, brown sugar, and cinnamon and turn heat to medium.

7. Stirring frequently, cook until the mangoes have slightly softened and the mixture is thick and gooey, 6 to 8 minutes.

8. Remove the mango mixture from heat and stir in the butter.

9. Spoon the mango mixture into wonton cups, about 3 tablespoons each. Top with coconut flakes (if using) and serve warm.

Nutrition: calories: 61; total fat 1g; saturated fat: 0g; cholesterol: 2mg; sodium: 52mg; potassium: 77mg; total carbohydrate: 14g; fiber: 1g; protein: 1g

83. Grilled Peach Sundaes

Preparation time: 15 minutes

Cooking time: 5 minutes

Servings: 1

Ingredients:

- 1 tbsp. Toasted unsweetened coconut

- 1 tsp. Canola oil

- 2 peaches, halved and pitted

- 2 scoops non-fat vanilla yogurt, frozen

Directions:

1. Brush the peaches with oil and grill until tender.

2. Place peach halves on a bowl and top with frozen yogurt and coconut.

Nutrition:

Calories: 61; carbs: 2g; protein: 2g; fats: 6g; phosphorus: 32mg; potassium: 85mg; sodium: 30mg

84. Blueberry Swirl Cake

Preparation time: 15 minutes

Cooking time: 45 minutes

Servings: 9

Ingredients:

- 1/2 cup margarine

- 1 1/4 cups reduced fat almond milk

- 1 cup granulated sugar

- 1 egg

- 1 egg white

- 1 tbsp. Lemon zest, grated

- 1 tsp. Cinnamon

- 1/3 cup light brown sugar

- 2 1/2 cups fresh blueberries

- 2 1/2 cups self-rising flour

Directions:

1. Cream the margarine and granulated sugar using an electric mixer at high speed until fluffy.

2. Add the egg and egg white and beat for another two minutes.

3. Add the lemon zest and reduce the speed to low.

4. Add the flour with almond milk alternately.

5. In a greased 13x19 pan, spread half of the batter and sprinkle with blueberry on top. Add the remaining batter.

6. Bake in a 350-degree Fahrenheit preheated oven for 45 minutes.

7. Let it cool on a wire rack before slicing and serving.

Nutrition:

Calories: 384; carbs: 63g; protein: 7g; fats: 13g; phosphorus: 264mg; potassium: 158mg; sodium: 456mg

85. Mixed Berry Cobbler

Preparation time: 15 minutes

Cooking time: 4 hours

Servings: 8

Ingredients:

- 1/4 cup coconut almond milk
- 1/4 cup ghee
- 1/4 cup honey

- 1/2 cup almond flour

- 1/2 cup tapioca starch

- 1/2 tablespoon cinnamon

- 1/2 tablespoon coconut sugar

- 1 teaspoon vanilla

- 12 ounces frozen raspberries

- 16 ounces frozen wild blueberries

- 2 teaspoon baking powder

- 2 teaspoon tapioca starch

Directions:

1. Place the frozen berries in the slow cooker. Add honey and 2 teaspoons of tapioca starch. Mix to combine.

2. In a bowl, mix the tapioca starch, almond flour, coconut almond milk, ghee, baking powder and vanilla. Sweeten with sugar. Place this pastry mix on top of the berries.

3. Set the slow cooker for 4 hours.

Nutrition:

Calories: 146; carbs: 33g; protein: 1g; fats: 3g; phosphorus: 29mg; potassium: 133mg; sodium: 4mg

86. Blueberry Espresso Brownies

Preparation time: 15 minutes

Cooking time: 30 minutes

Servings: 12

Ingredients:

- 1/4 cup organic cocoa powder
- 1/4 teaspoon salt
- 1/2 cup raw honey
- 1/2 teaspoon baking soda
- 1 cup blueberries
- 1 cup coconut cream
- 1 tablespoon cinnamon
- 1 tablespoon ground coffee
- 2 teaspoon vanilla extract
- 3 eggs

Directions:

1. Preheat the oven to 3250f.
2. In a bow mix together coconut cream, honey, eggs, cinnamon, honey, vanilla, baking soda, coffee and salt.
3. Use a mixer to combine all ingredients.
4. Fold in the blueberries
5. Pour the batter in a greased baking dish and bake for 30 minutes or until a toothpick inserted in the middle comes out clean.
6. Remove from the oven and let it cool.

Nutrition: Calories: 168; carbs: 20g; protein: 4g; fats: 10g; phosphorus: 79mg; potassium: 169mg; sodium: 129mg

87. Spiced Peaches

Preparation time: 5 minutes

Cooking time: 10 minutes

Servings: 2 servings

Ingredients:

- Peaches – 1 cup Cornstarch –
- ½ tsp. Ground cloves
- 1 tsp. Ground cinnamon
- 1 tsp. Ground nutmeg
- 1 tsp.Zest of ½ lemon
- Water ½ cup

Directions:

1. Combine cinnamon, cornstarch, nutmeg, ground cloves, and lemon zest in a pan on the stove.
2. Heat on a medium heat and add peaches.
3. Bring to a boil, reduce the heat and simmer for 10 minutes.
4. Serve.

Nutrition: calories: 70; fat: 0g; carb: 14g; phosphorus: 23mg; potassium: 176mg; sodium: 3mg; protein: 1g

88. Pumpkin Cheesecake Bar

Preparation time: 10 minutes

Cooking time: 50 minutes

Servings: 4 servings

Ingredients:

- Unsalted butter – 2 ½ tbsps.
- Cream cheese – 4 oz.
- All-purpose white flour – ½ cup
- Golden brown sugar – 3 tbsps.
- Granulated sugar – ¼ cup
- Pureed pumpkin – ½ cup
- Egg whites - 2
- Ground cinnamon – 1 tsp.
- Ground nutmeg – 1 tsp.
- Vanilla extract – 1 tsp.

Directions:

1. Preheat the oven to 350f.
2. Mix flour and brown sugar in a bowl.
3. Mix in the butter to form 'breadcrumbs.
4. Place ¾ of this mixture in a dish.
5. Bake in the oven for 15 minutes. Remove and cool.
6. Lightly whisk the egg and fold in the cream cheese, sugar, pumpkin, cinnamon, nutmeg and vanilla until smooth.
7. Pour this mixture over the oven-baked base and sprinkle with the rest of the breadcrumbs from earlier.

8. Bake in the oven for 30 to 35 minutes more.

9. Cool, slice and serve.

Nutrition: calories: 248; fat: 13g; carb: 33g; phosphorus: 67mg; potassium: 96mg; sodium: 146mg; protein: 4g

89. Blueberry Mini Muffins

Preparation time: 10 minutes

Cooking time: 35 minutes

Servings: 4 servings

Ingredients:

- Egg whites – 3
- All-purpose white flour – ¼ cup
- Coconut flour – 1 tbsp.
- Baking soda – 1 tsp.
- Nutmeg – 1 tbsp.
- Grated Vanilla extract – 1 tsp.
- Stevia – 1 tsp.
- Fresh blueberries – ¼ cup

Directions:

1. Preheat the oven to 325f.

2. Mix all the ingredients in a bowl.

3. Divide the batter into 4 and spoon into a lightly oiled muffin tin.

4. Bake in the oven for 15 to 20 minutes or until cooked through.

5. Cool and serve.

Nutrition: calories: 62; fat: 0g; carb: 9g; phosphorus: 103mg; potassium: 65mg; sodium: 62mg; protein: 4g;

90. Strawberry Ice Cream

Preparation time: 5 minutes

Cooking time: 5 minutes

Servings: 3 servings

Ingredients:

- Stevia – ½ cup

- Lemon juice – 1 tbsp.

- Non-dairy coffee creamer – ¾ cup

- Strawberries – 10 oz.

- Crushed ice – 1 cup

Directions:

1. Blend everything in a blend until smooth.

2. Freeze until frozen.

3. Serve.

Nutrition: calories: 94.4; fat: 6g; carb: 8.3g; phosphorus: 25mg; potassium: 108mg; sodium: 25mg; protein: 1.3g;

91. Cinnamon Custard

Preparation time: 20 minutes

Cooking time: 1 hour

Servings: 6 servings

Ingredients:

- Unsalted butter, for greasing the ramekins Plain rice almond milk – 1 ½ cups

- Eggs – 4

- Granulated sugar – ¼ cup

- Pure vanilla extract – 1 tsp.

- Ground cinnamon – ½ tsp.

- Cinnamon sticks for garnish

Directions:

1. Preheat the oven to 325f.

2. Lightly grease 6 ramekins and place them in a baking dish. Set aside.

3. In a large bowl, whisk together the eggs, rice almond milk, sugar, vanilla, and cinnamon until the mixture is smooth.

4. Pour the mixture through a fine sieve into a pitcher.

5. Evenly divide the custard mixture among the ramekins.

6. Fill the baking dish with hot water, until the water reaches halfway up the ramekins' sides.

7. Bake for 1 hour or until the custards are set and a knife inserted in the center comes out clean.

8. Remove the custards from the oven and take the ramekins out of the water.

9. Cool on the wire racks for 1 hour then chill for 1 hour.

10. garnish with cinnamon sticks and serve.

Nutrition: calories: 110; fat: 4g; carb: 14g; phosphorus: 100mg; potassium: 64mg; sodium: 71mg; protein: 4g;

92. Raspberry Brule

Preparation time: 15 minutes

Cooking time: 1 minute

Servings: 4 servings

Ingredients:

- Light sour cream – ½ cup
- Plain cream cheese – ½ cup
- Brown sugar – ¼ cup,
- divided Ground cinnamon – ¼ tsp.
- Fresh raspberries – 1 cup

Directions:

1. Preheat the oven to broil.

2. In a bowl, beat together the cream cheese, sour cream, 2 tbsp. Brown sugar and cinnamon for 4 minutes or until the mixture is very smooth and fluffy.

3. Evenly divide the raspberries among 4 (4-ounce) ramekins.

4. Spoon the cream cheese mixture over the berries and smooth the tops.

5. Sprinkle ½ tbsp. Brown sugar evenly over each ramekin.

6. Place the ramekins on a baking sheet and broil 4 inches from the heating element until the sugar is caramelized and golden brown.

7. Cool and serve.

Nutrition: **calories:** 188; fat: 13g; carb: 16g; phosphorus: 60mg; potassium: 158mg; sodium: 132mg; protein

93. Gingerbread Loaf

Preparation time: 20 minutes

Cooking time: 1 hour

Servings: 16

Ingredients:

- Unsalted butter, for greasing the baking dish 3 cups all-purpose flour
- ½ teaspoon ener-g baking soda substitute
- 2 teaspoons ground cinnamon
- 1 teaspoon ground allspice
- ¾ cup granulated sugar
- 1¼ cups plain rice almond milk
- 1 large egg
- ¼ cup olive oil
- 2 tablespoons molasses
- 2 teaspoons grated fresh ginger
- Powdered sugar, for dusting

Directions:

1. Preheat the oven to 350°f.

2. Lightly grease a 9-by-13-inch baking dish with butter; set aside.

3. In a large bowl, sift together the flour, baking soda substitute, cinnamon, and allspice.

4. Stir the sugar into the flour mixture.

5. In medium bowl, whisk together the almond milk, egg, olive oil,

6. molasses, and ginger until well blended.

7. Make a well in the center of the flour mixture and pour in the wet ingredients.

8. Mix until just combined, taking care not to overmix.

9. Pour the batter into the baking dish and bake for about 1 hour or until a wooden pick inserted in the middle comes out clean.

10. Serve warm with a dusting of powdered sugar.

Nutrition: calories: 232; fat: 5g; carbohydrates: 42g; phosphorus: 54mg; potassium: 104mg; sodium: 18mg; protein: 4g

94. Elegant Lavender Cookies

preparation time: 10 minutes

Cooking time: 15 minutes

Servings: makes 24 cookies

Ingredients:

- 5 dried organic lavender flowers, the entire top of the flower
- ½ cup granulated sugar
- 1 cup unsalted butter, at room temperature
- 2 cups all-purpose flour
- 1 cup rice flour

Directions:

1. Strip the tiny lavender flowers off the main stem carefully and place the flowers and granulated sugar into a food processor or blender. Pulse until the mixture is finely chopped.

2. In a medium bowl, cream together the butter and lavender sugar until it is very fluffy.

3. Mix the flours into the creamed mixture until the mixture resembles fine crumbs.

4. Gather the dough together into a ball and then roll it into a long log.

5. Wrap the cookie dough in plastic and refrigerate it for about 1 hour or until firm.

6. Preheat the oven to 375°f.

7. Slice the chilled dough into ¼-inch rounds and refrigerate it for 1 hour or until firm.

8. Bake the cookies for 15 to 18 minutes or until they are a very pale, golden brown.

9. Let the cookies cool.

10. Store the cookies at room temperature in a sealed container for up to 1 week.

Nutrition: calories: 153; fat: 9g; carbohydrates: 17g; phosphorus: 18mg; potassium: 17mg; sodium: 0mg; protein: 1g

95. Carob Angel Food Cake

preparation time: 30 minutes

Cooking time: 30 minutes

Servings: 16

Ingredients:

- ¾ cup all-purpose flour
- ¼ cup carob flour
- 1½ cups sugar, divided
- 12 large egg whites, at room temperature
- 1½ teaspoons cream of tartar
- 2 teaspoons vanilla

Directions:

1. Preheat the oven to 375°f.

2. In a medium bowl, sift together the all-purpose flour, carob flour, and ¾ cup of the sugar; set aside.

3. Beat the egg whites and cream of tartar with a hand mixer for about 5 minutes or until soft peaks form.

4. Add the remaining ¾ cup sugar by the tablespoon to the egg whites until all the sugar is used up and stiff peaks form.

5. Fold in the flour mixture and vanilla.

6. Spoon the batter into an angel food cake pan.

7. Run a knife through the batter to remove any air pockets.

8. Bake the cake for about 30 minutes or until the top springs back when pressed lightly.

9. Invert the pan onto a wire rack to cool.

10. Run a knife around the rim of the cake pan and remove the cake from the pan.

Nutrition: calories: 113; fat: 0g; carbohydrates: 25g; phosphorus: 11mg; potassium: 108mg; sodium: 42mg; protein: 3g

96. Old-Fashioned Apple Kuchen

preparation time: 25 minutes

Cook time: 1 hour

Servings: 16

Ingredients:

- Unsalted butter, for greasing the baking dish

- 1 cup unsalted butter, at room temperature

- 2 cups granulated sugar

- 2 eggs, beaten

- 2 teaspoons pure vanilla extract

- 2 cups all-purpose flour

- 1 teaspoon ener-g baking soda substitute

- 2 teaspoons ground cinnamon

- ½ teaspoon ground nutmeg Pinch ground allspice

- 2 large apples, peeled, cored, and diced (about 3 cups)

Directions:

1. Preheat the oven to 350°f.

2. Grease a 9-by-13-inch glass baking dish; set aside.

3. Cream together the butter and sugar with a hand mixer until light and fluffy, for about 3 minutes.

4. Add the eggs and vanilla and beat until combined, scraping down the sides of the bowl, about 1 minute.

5. In a small bowl, stir together the flour, baking soda substitute, cinnamon, nutmeg, and allspice.

6. Add the dry ingredients to the wet ingredients and stir to combine.

7. Stir in the apple and spoon the batter into the baking dish.

8. Bake for about 1 hour or until the cake is golden.

9. Cool the cake on a wire rack.

10. Serve warm or chilled.

Nutrition: calories: 368; fat: 16g; carbohydrates: 53g; phosphorus: 46mg; potassium: 68mg; sodium: 15mg; protein: 3g

97. Dessert Cocktail

Preparation time: 1 minutes

Cooking time: 0 minute

Servings: 4

Ingredients:
- 1 cup of cranberry juice
- 1 cup of fresh ripe strawberries, washed and hull removed
- 2 tablespoon of lime juice
- ¼ cup of white sugar
- 8 ice cubes

Directions:

1. Combine all the ingredients in a blender until smooth and creamy.

2. Pour the liquid into chilled tall glasses and serve cold.

Nutrition: Calories: 92 kcal Carbohydrate: 23.5 g Protein: 0.5 g Sodium: mg Potassium: 103.78 mg Phosphorus: 17.86 mg Dietary fiber: 0.84 g Fat: 0.17 g

98. Baked Egg Custard

Preparation time: 15 minutes

Cooking time: 30 minutes

Servings: 4

Ingredients:

- 2 medium eggs, at room temperature
- ¼ cup of semi-skimmed almond milk
- 3 tablespoons of white sugar
- ½ teaspoon of nutmeg
- 1 teaspoon of vanilla extract

Directions:

1. Preheat your oven at 375 f/180c
2. Mix all the ingredients in a mixing bowl and beat with a hand mixer for a few seconds until creamy and uniform.
3. Pour the mixture into lightly greased muffin tins.
4. Bake for 25-30 minutes or until the knife, you place inside, comes out clean.

Nutrition: Calories: 96.56 kcal Carbohydrate: 10.5 g Protein: 3.5 g Sodium: 37.75 mg Potassium: 58.19 mg Phosphorus: 58.76 mg Dietary fiber: 0.06 g Fat: 2.91 g

99. Easy Fudge

Preparation time: 15 minutes + chill time

Cooking time: 5 minutes

Servings: 25

Ingredients

- 1 ¾ cups of coconut butter
- 1 cup pumpkin puree
- 1 teaspoon ground cinnamon
- ¼ teaspoon ground nutmeg
- 1 tablespoon coconut oil

Directions

- Take an 8x8 inch square baking pan and line it with aluminum foil
- Take a spoon and scoop out the coconut butter into a heated pan and allow the butter to melt
- Keep stirring well and remove from the heat once fully melted
- Add spices and pumpkin and keep straining until you have a grain- like texture
- Add coconut oil and keep stirring to incorporate everything
- Scoop the mixture into your baking pan and evenly distribute it

- Place wax paper on top of the mixture and press gently to straighten the top

- Remove the paper and discard

- Allow it to chill for 1-2 hours

- Once chilled, take it out and slice it up into pieces

- Enjoy!

Nutrition: calories: 120 fats: 10g carbohydrates: 5g protein: 1.2g Phosphorus: 88mg Potassium: 90mg Sodium: 75mg

100. Coconut Loaf

Preparation time: 15 minutes

Cooking time: 40 minutes

Servings: 4

Ingredients

- 1 ½ tablespoons coconut flour

- ¼ teaspoon baking powder

- 1/8 teaspoon salt

- 1 tablespoon coconut oil, melted

- 1 whole egg

Directions

1. Preheat your oven to 350 °f

2. Add coconut flour, baking powder, salt

3. Add coconut oil, eggs and stir well until mixed

4. Leave the batter for several minutes

5. Pour half the batter onto the baking pan

6. Spread it to form a circle, repeat with remaining batter

7. Bake in the oven for 10 minutes

8. Once a golden-brown texture comes, let it cool and serve

9. Enjoy!

Nutrition: calories: 297 fats: 14g carbohydrates: 15g protein: 15g Phosphorus: 80mg Potassium: 97mg Sodium: 75mg

101. Cashew Cheese Bites

Preparation Time: 5 minutes

Cooking Time: 5 minutes

Servings: 12

Ingredients:

- 8 oz cream cheese

- 1 tsp cinnamon

- 1 cup cashew butter

Directions:

1. Add all ingredients into the blender and blend until smooth.

2. Pour blended mixture into the mini muffin liners and place them in the refrigerator until set.

3. Serve and enjoy.

Nutrition: Calories 192 Fat 17.1 g Carbohydrates 6.5 g Sugar 0 g Protein 5.2 g Cholesterol 21 mg Phosphorus: 110mg Potassium: 117mg Sodium: 75mg

102. Healthy Cinnamon Lemon Tea

Preparation Time: 5 minutes

Cooking Time: 5 minutes

Servings: 1

Ingredients:

- 1/2 tbsp fresh lemon juice
- 1 cup of water
- 1 tsp ground cinnamon

Directions:

1. Add water in a saucepan and bring to boil over medium heat.
2. Add cinnamon and stir to cinnamon dissolve.
3. Add lemon juice and stir well.
4. Serve hot.

Nutrition: Calories 9 Fat 0.2 g Carbohydrates 2 g Sugar 0.3 g Protein 0.2 g Cholesterol 0 mg Phosphorus: 70mg Potassium: 87mg Sodium: 65mg

103. Detoxifying Beet Juice

Preparation Time: 10 minutes

Cooking Time: 10 minutes

Servings: 4

Ingredients:

- 1-pound beets, washed with ends cut off

- 2 pounds carrots, washed with ends cut off

- 1 bunch celery, washed and broken into ribs

- 2 lemons, peel cut off and quartered

- 1 lime, peel cut off and quartered

- 1 bunch flat-leaf parsley, washed

- 1 Fuji or Honeycrisp red apple, chopped (optional, for extra sweetness)

Directions:

1. Wash produces and chop so pieces will fit into the feeder tube of your juicer.

2. Feed the vegetable pieces through the juicer, alternating harder and softer textured pieces to aid in the juicing process.

3. Serve immediately or store in the refrigerator in a highly sealed container.

4. The juice is best when served within 48 hours of making.

Nutrition: Calories: 58 Fat: 0g Carbs: 13g Protein: 2g Sodium: 106mg Potassium: 442mg Phosphorus: 54mg

104. Honey Cinnamon Latte

Preparation Time: 5 minutes

Cooking Time: 5 minutes

Servings: 2 Ingredients:

- 1-½ cups of organic, unsweetened almond milk
- 1 scoop of organic vanilla protein powder
- 1 teaspoon of organic cinnamon
- ½ teaspoon of pure, local honey
- 1-2 shots of espresso

Directions:

1. Heat almond milk in the microwave until hot to the touch.
2. Add honey and stir until completely melted.
3. Using a whisk, add cinnamon, and protein powder and thoroughly combine.
4. Pour into a manual milk and froth concoction until foamy and creamy.
5. Pour espresso shots into a mug and add in milk mixture.

Nutrition: Calories: 115 Fat: 3g Carbs: 26g Protein: 3g Sodium: 125mg Potassium: 10.9mg Phosphorus: 0.1mg

105. Cinnamon Smoothie

Preparation Time: 5 minutes

Cooking Time: 5 minutes

Servings: 2

Ingredients:

- 150g plain or Greek yogurt
- 300ml milk
- 2 tbsp smooth peanut butter
- 1/4 tsp Schwartz Ground Cinnamon

Directions:

1. Add all the ingredients to a blender and blitz until smooth.
2. Serve immediately.

Nutrition: Calories: 88 Fat: 4.3g Carbs: 3g Protein: 8g Sodium: 187mg Potassium: 241mg Phosphorus: 20mg

106. Citrus Smoothie

Preparation Time: 5 minutes

Cooking Time: 2 minutes

Servings: 2

Ingredients:

- 1 large orange, peeled, halved
- ¼ lemon, peeled, seeded
- ½ cup (85 g) pineapple, peeled, cubed

- ¼ cup (60 g) frozen mango

- 1 cup (130 g) ice cubes

Directions:

1. Prepare all ingredients into the container and secure lid.

2. Turn machine on and slowly increase speed to high.

3. Blend for 1 minute or until the desired consistency is reached.

Nutrition: Calories: 280 Fat: 0g Carbs: 67g Protein: 4g Sodium: 30mg Potassium: 570mg Phosphorus: 0mg